SEARCHING THE SCRIPTURES

SOCIETY OF BIBLICAL LITERATURE
BIBLICAL SCHOLARSHIP IN NORTH AMERICA

Kent Harold Richards, Editor

NUMBER 8
SEARCHING THE SCRIPTURES
A History of the Society of Biblical Literature,
1880–1980
Ernest W. Saunders

ERNEST W. SAUNDERS

SEARCHING THE SCRIPTURES
A History of the Society of Biblical Literature,
1880–1980

SCHOLARS PRESS
Chico, California

The Society of Biblical Literature gratefully acknowledges a grant from the National Endowment for the Humanities to underwrite certain editorial and research expenses of the Centennial Publications Series. Published results and interpretations do not necessarily represent the view of the Endowment.

Library of Congress Cataloging in Publication Data

Saunders, Ernest W.
    Searching the Scriptures.

    (Biblical scholarship in North America ; no. 8)
    (Centennial publications / Society of Biblical Literature)
    Includes bibliographical references and index.
    1. Society of Biblical Literature—History.   I. Title.
II. Series. II. Series: Centennial publications (Society of Biblical Literature)
BS411.S622S38   1982   220'.06'07   82–10818
ISBN 0–89130–591–2

Printed in the United States of America

To the Society of Biblical Literature,
Respectfully and
Affectionately Submitted

ERNEST W. SAUNDERS is a well-known lecturer and writer in the fields of New Testament literature, its Roman-Hellenistic cultural environment, and textual criticism. He is professor emeritus of New Testament Interpretation and former dean of Garrett-Evangelical Theological Seminary in Evanston, Illinois.

Professor Saunders has been a member of the Society of Biblical Literature for forty-one years. He has served as the Society's Honorary President and as a delegate to the American Council of Learned Societies.

TABLE OF CONTENTS

Illustrations

PREFACE

This is the story of a group of people, dedicated to teaching and research, who have influenced significantly the course of American biblical scholarship for over a century. Some of them are well known beyond the circle of professional colleagues; others are familiar only to immediate associates and students. Their academic discipline of critical study of the Jewish and Christian scriptures is among the oldest in the panoply of the fields of knowledge. Their Society ranks among the oldest of academic associations in the area of humanistic studies in North America. Its members are drawn from faculties of religious studies in undergraduate colleges and universities and graduate schools of religion in the United States and Canada. It declares itself to the larger community of scholars in these terms:

> The object of the Society is to stimulate the critical investigation of the classical biblical literatures, together with other related literature, by the exchange of scholarly research both in published form and in public forum. The Society endeavors to support those disciplines and subdisciplines pertinent to the illumination of the literatures and religions of the ancient Near Eastern and Mediterranean regions, such as the study of ancient languages, textual criticism, history, and archaeology.

The completion of the first century of service to biblical research affords occasion to reflect upon and to assess the work of the Society to date and to determine future direction. That past, however, has all too often been minimized in relationship to the older and allegedly richer contribution of European scholarship in this field. In consequence there has been only minor interest in that history and its impact on American culture as well as on international scholarship. In truth, as Roy A. Harrisville has written in his critical study of one of the pioneers in American biblical interpretation, "A man ought to know who he was before he dies. Those years of scholarly activity in this country, extending roughly from 1890 to 1940, give identity to many of us responsible for biblical studies here. And in many ways, those years were our better part—they marked an eminently fruitful period in American scholarship, and in the opinion of some, the most fruitful to date."° Those years, enclosing Frank Chamberlain Porter's lifetime, prepared for the latest forty-year period, in which American biblical studies

---

° *Frank Chamberlain Porter, Pioneer in American Biblical Interpretation* (Missoula: Scholars Press, 1976) v, vi.

have come of age. In the opinion of others, though, we who are alive to tell may think more highly of ourselves than we ought.

In any event, this is a biographical study of an organization, and as such it is subject to pride and prejudice, but, I hope, also to probity. The account is gleaned from many disparate sources. Prior to 1960 records are woefully sparse, especially for the 'first forty years. Beyond the proceedings and papers published in the *Journal*, information about the period up to 1960 is scattered about in the *CSR Bulletin*, *Scholia*, programs of annual meetings, mimeographed committee reports, minutes, budgets, secretaries' notes, and business files. The whole represents a cross between the *Congressional Record* and the *New York City Telephone Directory*. More revealing are the incidents lodged in living memories and personal correspondence. One friend and member wrote at the outset of this project, "Unless the anecdotal history of the SBL can be recovered, you could produce the dullest book since the Book of Chronicles." Another in a more cynical vein cautioned, "I fear that the proposed history will turn out to be the sort of white-washed sepulchre commonly used for such occasions." There are plenty of dry bones here, no doubt. One can only hope that for some, at least, they may yet live.

Those who have contributed records and recollections to the writing of this story are numbered beyond naming. I am especially indebted to certain persons who supplied material aid, comfort, criticism, and guidance to the study. Their assistance I gratefully acknowledge: R. Lansing Hicks, John T. Fitzgerald, Jr., Thomas H. Olbricht, Charles Karsten, Elizabeth Wiggins, Amos N. Wilder, Edward R. Hardy, David Hopkins and Ann E. Millin of Vanderbilt Divinity School Library, Seth Kasten of Union Theological Seminary Library in New York, Maria Grossmann of Andover-Harvard Theological Library, Pierson Parker of the Center for Biblical Research and Archives at Claremont, Robert W. Funk, and Robert Kraft (son of a former executive secretary), to whom we are all indebted for the discovery of two priceless manuscript volumes of secretarial records. Every reader is benefited by the thirty-five senior scholars who responded generously to an invitation to share reminiscences and anecdotes out of their extended association with the Society. Pictures of the charter members were contributed by Thomas H. Olbricht. The manuscript was read critically by Paul J. Achtemeier, Dorothy C. Bass, Philip J. King, Harry M. Orlinsky and was strengthened by their suggestions. I tender special thanks to Executive Secretary Kent Harold Richards for his cheerful assistance in sending files and other papers to me in the Maine woods and for his willingness to supervise the passage of the manuscript from desk to press. His substantive contributions as the editor of this volume along with the tireless work of Maurya P. Horgan were most appreciated. Though resolute effort has been made for accuracy in retrieval and report, I must accept responsibility for what remains imperfect.

I

IN THE BEGINNING, 1880-1900

Setting

The educational system in the United States in the second half of the nineteenth century was marked by rapid growth, feverish activity, and sharp collision between secular and ecclesiastical forces in contest for control. In the northeastern section of the country this was especially evident where the swelling tide of European immigrants severely taxed the limited resources of the newly established public school systems. Conservative church leaders in the revivalist tradition deplored the secularization of the curricula and struggled to develop a parallel parochial program, a response that is repeating itself today. Then, as now, at issue was the dominance of a world view that was perceived to be alien to the world view of the Jewish and Christian scriptures and hence was a lethal threat to faith. It was not simply the minuscule role that religious instruction was permitted to play in the school curriculum that aroused the criticisms of church leaders. That was deplorable enough. What infuriated them was the teaching of a scientific naturalism, imported from Europe, that was perceived to be diametrically opposed to the biblical doctrine of creation and made no place for redemption other than by human achievement. The battle was to intensify and culminate in the Fundamentalist controversies of the twenties.

New winds were blowing in Europe and many feared they would gather strength to gale force by the time they reached the western shores. It was an age of new research and exciting discoveries in all areas of human knowledge. Michael Faraday, Charles Darwin, Thomas Huxley, Louis Pasteur, and Joseph Lister were exploding earlier conceptions in the physical sciences, matched by Karl Marx, Thomas Carlyle, G. W. F. Hegel, Auguste Comte, and F. W. Nietzsche in the social sciences and philosophy. Some greeted the new naturalism (was there any room left for the supernatural?) with terror and dismay. Others, undaunted, believed that it marked the end of old tyrannies by the church and other authoritarian institutions and the beginning of a new freedom. To call the names of Ferdinand Christian Baur, Hermann Gunkel, David Friedrich Strauss, and Julius Wellhausen is to recall formidable biblical scholars who became purveyors of the new scientific spirit that challenged the axioms of biblical traditionalism and opened up exciting, if disturbing, new approaches to an understanding of scripture. "By 1900, every traditional Christian doctrine had been subjected to a devastating review in terms of the new, non-biblical knowledge—from cosmology to eschatology, from the Bible as the literally inerrant locus of revelation to the Church as a divine institution among men."[1]

Nor is it to be forgotten that the time was one of social as well as intellectual upheaval. The disastrous Civil War, of recent memory, was followed by social turbulence. The ordered society of New England was disrupted by the daily arrivals of immigrants from Europe looking for a new life but often caught in ethnic strife in the cities where they settled. Powerful political bosses and business robber barons held sway, but workers were rising in struggle to organize for the protection of their own rights in a developing industrial society.

In such a society the organization of a group of teachers and clergy dedicated to classical learning, specifically learning focused on the literature of the Bible, went unnoticed except for the corporal's guard of those who enlisted. Such gatherings of gentle folk who hoped among other things to belie the American image abroad and show themselves to be suitably educated patrons of culture and learning had become popular in the earlier part of the century. These societies, as they were termed, were usually composed of scholars of independent means, scientists, and amateurs who enjoyed common interests of learning and who shared their views with a larger public, as in the famous lyceums where Ralph Waldo Emerson and Henry David Thoreau lectured. Out of these emerged esoteric groups more specialized and academic and restricted to professional scholars. Admission to these associations carried the minimum requirement of enrollment in a graduate seminar, itself inspired by the German university system. Pride of place was accorded the American Philosophical Society, founded in 1743. The American Antiquarian Society began to meet in 1812; the numismatists organized in 1858 and the venerable American Oriental Society, colleague of the Society of Biblical Literature and Exegesis, held its first meeting in 1842. In the post–Civil War period one followed upon another: the American Philological Association, 1869; the American Social Science Association, 1869; the Archaeological Institute of America, 1879; the Modern Language Association, 1883; and the American Historical Society in 1884.

In short order these newly organized associations began to publish scholarly journals in keeping with models set by the European societies, thus entering the ongoing debate of problems of scholarship in their respective disciplines. A few examples will suffice. The *Transactions of the American Philological Association* began publication in 1869 and the *Journal* in 1880.

---

[1] David L. Dungan, "The Present State of the SBL and the History of American Biblical Interpretation," an unpublished paper read at the one hundred and fourth annual meeting of the SBL, 1968.

The former year saw the initial publication of the *Journal of the American Social Science Association*. The Society of Biblical Archaeology began to publish its *Proceedings* in 1878. The *Transactions of the Modern Language Association* appeared in 1884; the *Papers of the American Historical Association* in 1886; the *Philosophical Review* in 1892; and the *American Journal of Theology* in 1897. Into this distinguished company, the *Journal of Biblical Literature and Exegesis* made its entrance in 1881. Not only did these journals give a new recognition to the American scholar; they also shaped the directions of research in their fields and profoundly influenced the character of seminary and university scholarship and instruction.

Origins and Early Years

Sources for a knowledge of the preparation and early meetings of the first inter-school association for biblical studies—to be known as the Society of Biblical Literature and Exegesis[2]—are scanty, confined largely to the records of the Council and the annual meetings. It appears that Frederic Gardiner of Berkeley Divinity School in Middletown, Connecticut, initiated conversations with Philip Schaff and Charles Augustus Briggs of Union Theological Seminary in New York about the need for such a group. The outcome was a preliminary meeting held in Schaff's study in New York City on the second of January, 1880, "to take into consideration the formation of a Society for the promotion of study in Biblical Literature and Exegesis."[3] Eight persons attended. In addition to Gardiner, Schaff, and Briggs there were Daniel Raynes Goodwin of the Episcopal Divinity School in Philadelphia, Charles Short of Columbia University, James Strong of Drew Theological Seminary, and two pastors, Jacob I. Mombert of Passaic, New Jersey, and E. A. Washburn of New York City. There were older study groups, such as the Harvard Biblical Club, already in existence, but this was the first association of teachers and clergy on an inter-school and inter-confessional basis. Though based in the Northeast for many years, it would early widen its membership geographically and denominationally.

The group drew up a preliminary list of seventeen persons to be invited into membership, appointed Gardiner, Briggs, Short, and Strong to constitute a committee to plan the first meeting on 4 June and to draft a constitution and by-laws to be presented at that meeting. In a letter to Briggs, written several weeks later, Gardiner observed that the by-laws, evidently his work, were adaptations of those of the American Oriental Society. Indicative of Gardiner's interest in drawing conservative scholars into the discussion, the Middletown scholar noted his efforts to enlist into membership Princeton professors C. A. Aiken, W. H. Green, Charles W. Hodge (chief figure in

---

[2] Also referred to as the SBL. The original title was shortened in 1962 to the Society of Biblical Literature.

[3] See Appendix I, Manuscript Record of the Preliminary Meeting, 2 January 1880.

Protestant scholasticism, the conservative theologian alleged to have said, "a new idea never originated in Princeton"), and James F. McCurdy. McCurdy accepted only to withdraw subsequently. In May, the announcement was sent to a list of thirty-five persons who had signified their interest in joining:

> The first meeting of the Society of Biblical Literature and Exegesis will be held in New York at the study of Rev. Dr. Washburn, Rector of Calvary Church, 103 East 21st St., N.Y. on Friday, June 4th at 2 p.m. for the purpose of organization and of the reading and discussion of papers. Frederic Gardiner, sect. *pro tem.* (C. A. Briggs, *Letters* V, #1206, 408)

Eighteen persons attended the first meeting of the Society on 4 and 5 June (see figure 1).[4] They adopted a constitution and by-laws (which curiously omitted any statement of purpose), elected officers, and heard Philip Schaff read a paper ("The Pentecostal and the Corinthian Glossolalia"), engaged in spirited discussion of five other papers, and adjourned until the next meeting on 30 December. Goodwin, former provost of the University of Pennsylvania, was chosen to head the new organization. Strong, who was later to edit the *Exhaustive Concordance of the Bible* (1895), was named vice-president. Gardiner, who had been temporary secretary, became continuing secretary, and C. A. Briggs, stout advocate of the new biblical science and partner with Francis Brown and Samuel Rolles Driver in the monumental *Hebrew and English Lexicon of the Old Testament*, was named treasurer. A council of nine—the officers and Ezra Abbot, George E. Day, Timothy Dwight, Charles Short, and E. A. Washburn—served as a steering committee.[5]

By the end of the year the fledgling Society ambitiously promised the publication of the proceedings and summaries of the papers in booklet form (which appeared in 1881) and boasted a membership of forty-five. In the earliest years the only criterion for membership that was defined, beyond a common interest in biblical studies, was the quality of the candidate's "exegetical writings," though this was never rigidly enforced. An initiation fee of five dollars entitled the new member to all the rights and privileges, and annual dues of three dollars kept one in good standing and insured receipt of any publications that were produced.

A year later the *Journal* was launched, published by Secretary Gardiner and Treasurer Briggs, who were given directions "to print the papers read at the June meeting (1881) in full and those of the December meeting as far as the funds would allow."[6] That pledge to publish papers in full was taken

---

[4] See Appendix I, Manuscript Record of the Preliminary Meeting, 2 January 1880.

[5] The proceedings and abstracts for the first two meetings 4–5 June 1880 and 30 December 1880, were printed and distributed in pamphlet form but were not included in the first volume of the *Journal* in 1881. They were reprinted in the semicentennial volume (50 [1931] xxiv–xlix). A collation with Gardiner's records, however, reveals variants.

[6] See further chapter VIII.

Ezra Abbot   Willis J. Beecher   Charles A. Briggs

Francis Brown   Daniel Raynes Goodwin   George E. Day

Joseph Henry Thayer   Crawford H. Toy   Philip Schaff

Figure 1. A Group of Charter Members

Center, Daniel Raynes Goodwin, first president of the SBL, 1880–1887.

seriously. Ezra Abbot's text-critical study of Romans 9:5, read at the fourth meeting, ran to sixty-seven pages in the first volume of the *Journal*!

Membership

A perusal of the roster of scholars who joined the Society in the first ten years reveals some interesting aspects of its growth and makeup. Familiar names in the history of American biblical and historical scholarship appear before their reputations have been established. Internationally known Syriac scholar Isaac H. Hall became a member in 1880. At the third meeting in 1881, Henry Preserved Smith of Lane Theological Seminary was a guest, joining the membership at the next meeting. We read of William Rainey Harper of the Baptist Theological Seminary of Morgan Park (Chicago), admitted at the fifth meeting in 1882. Conservatives were strengthened when Benjamin B. Warfield of Allegheny Seminary accepted membership (1882). George Foot Moore, teaching at Andover Theological Seminary at the time, joined in 1883 and exercised decisive leadership in the Society. When the decision was made in 1889 to create a new leadership post, to be termed corresponding secretary, with responsibility for program planning and chairing a committee to edit and publish the *Journal*, the Council chose Moore for the post. Over the next six years he was to bring his scholarly and editorial gifts to the service of the *Journal* and the Society. That same year also brought into the group Ernest DeWitt Burton, a man destined to play a decisive role with Harper in the famed "Chicago School." The cast of characters active in the following years extends to include other well-known personalities: James Rendel Harris of Baltimore; Caspar R. Gregory of Leipzig; Shailer Mathews of Colby College; Nathaniel Schmidt of Hamilton, New York; Benjamin W. Bacon of Lyme, Connecticut. The list constitutes a *Who's Who* in American biblical studies.

College, university, and seminary faculties were represented from the beginning. Half of the initial group of thirty-five were European trained in such universities as Berlin, Halle, and Tübingen. Through them German biblical science made its first impact on American scholarship and teaching.

Considering the strong regional character of the organization it is surprising to note the geographical spread of the membership in these early years. In the second year, the Reverend Canon Maurice S. Baldwin of Montreal enlisted in the ranks, the first Canadian in a Society that was increasingly to represent North American scholarship. At the initial meeting a paper prepared by the Reverend Robert Hutcheson of Washington, Iowa, was read posthumously. The cities of Cincinnati, Chicago, Baltimore, Nashville, Omaha, Denver, Pasadena, Oberlin, Montreal, Toronto, Leipzig, Osaka were represented by 1890, and the range widened in the next decade. Meeting places, of course, were centered in the Northeast but were not yet localized to New York City. Jewish scholarship is first represented by Rabbis

Marcus Jastrow, Gustav Gottheil, and his son Richard J. H. Gottheil who joined in 1886. However, attendance at the semiannual meetings in June and December was drawn from members living in the Northeast, averaging twenty.

An article in the revised constitution of 1889 provided for the election of honorary members outside the United States and Canada "distinguished for their attainments as Biblical scholars." Two years later, at the twenty-second meeting in 1891, the first group was chosen.[7] Named were William Sanday, Oxford; Charles John Ellicott, Bishop of Gloucester and Bristol; Brooke Foss Westcott, Bishop of Durham; Thomas Kelly Cheyne, Oxford; Bernhard Weiss, Berlin; Frédéric Godet, Neuchâtel; Carl Paul Caspari, Christiania (Oslo); August Dillmann, Berlin; Eberhard Schrader, Berlin; and Abraham Kuenen, Leiden.

Through the Society's first century the widening list of honorary members included the most creative and influential European scholars devoted to the study of ancient Near Eastern, biblical, and late Roman literature. They were frontier people whose work substantially advanced research in the field. Except for special occasions, never more than two were chosen each year, and for long stretches of time there were no nominations or elections. Strained relations between the Old World and the New account for the fact that none was chosen from 1913 to 1922 or from 1943 to 1945. In acknowledgment of their election, some members prepared articles which were published in the *Journal*, notably Karl Budde of Marburg, elected in 1898, who submitted nine contributions over a period of years. He also provided invaluable assistance in the printing of the *Journal* in Germany (1913–1934), especially during the war years.

The *Journal* records the passing of some of the first leaders. The 1884 meeting in Hartford memorialized Ezra Abbot as "one of the founders of the Society," and Charles Short was mourned in 1886. Frederic Gardiner, who seems to have been the prime mover of the Society, had served faithfully as its first secretary until ill health forced his resignation in 1883, but four years later he was elected the second president. He presided at the important nineteenth meeting in 1889 where significant constitutional changes were made that added the category of honorary members, divided the secretary's office into two parts (corresponding and recording), authorized the formation of regional groupings, and established an annual address by the president. A month later Gardiner was dead. The memorial resolution, adopted at the December meeting, acknowledged his influential role in the birth and earliest years of the Society. "Professor Gardiner was one of the original members of the Society. In fact, it was he who first suggested it, and who was chiefly instrumental in bringing together, June 4, 1880, in New York, the gentlemen who completed the organization" (*JBL* 9 [1890] vi[8]). He

[7] See Appendix II, Honorary Members.

[8] Hereafter references to the *Journal* will include volume, date, and page.

was not the most exciting teacher, according to the reports of some of his
students, nor was he renowned as an eminent scholar among his peers,
though he contributed nine articles and notes to the early volumes of the
Journal. But he was adept in organizational matters and he persisted stub-
bornly in transforming a plan for scholarly exchange into a structure. The
Society is his lengthened shadow. In Christ Church, Gardiner, Maine, his
ancestral home, a stained glass window given in 1920 by his missionary
daughter Henrietta memorializes Gardiner's life as a teacher and priest (see
figure 2). He is buried in the family lot in the adjacent yard. Oddly enough,
surviving members of his family, when interviewed, had no knowledge of
his relationship with the Society. But then, in those days it was a small circle
of professional friends getting together to discuss their work in a rector's
study or in a classroom. Contracting with Loews-Anatole Hotel in Dallas for
a centennial meeting was beyond the imagination of Society members at
that time.

Gardiner's long-time friend and colleague, Daniel Raynes Goodwin, sur-
vived him by less than a year; he died on 16 March 1890. A fellow Mainer
and Episcopal priest, Goodwin was the first president of the Society. He
contributed to the pages of the *Journal* ten notes reflecting his philological
interests. Beginning his teaching career at Bowdoin College as the successor
to his former teacher Henry Wadsworth Longfellow, Goodwin taught modern languages, moral and intellectual philosophy, apologetics, and systematic
divinity. A lifelong champion of the humanities, he fought unsuccessfully to
prevent the establishment of a faculty in science at the University of Pennsylvania while he was provost (1860–1868). Historian and philologist—
Gardiner and Goodwin together symbolize the dominant concerns of the
Society to the present day. Eleven of the first group of thirty-five were living in 1910, and one, David G. Lyon (1852–1935) lived to celebrate the
semicentennial anniversary of the Society in 1930.

The next decade introduced a number of younger scholars to the work
of the Society. Among them some names appear that are well known to later
generations: George A. Barton, who taught at Bryn Mawr College; Cyrus
Adler from the Johns Hopkins University; Frank Chamberlain Porter from
Yale Divinity School; Charles Cutler Torrey, who taught at Andover Seminary; James Hardy Ropes from Harvard; Charles Foster Kent from Brown;
James E. Frame, Arthur C. McGiffert, William Adams Brown, and Julius A.
Bewer from Union in New York; Walter Rauschenbusch from Rochester;
and Shailer Mathews and Edgar J. Goodspeed from Chicago. A few women
braved the male ranks; the first was Anna Ely Rhoads, who with a master's
degree from Bryn Mawr joined in 1894. Two years later she was joined by
Rebecca Corwin, who taught at Mount Holyoke College, and in 1898 by
Mary E. Woolley of Wellesley, later president of Mount Holyoke College.
Emilie Grace Briggs, a graduate of Union Theological Seminary in New
York and the daughter of Charles A. Briggs, was accepted into membership

Figure 2. Medallion in Memorial Window, Christ Church, Gardiner, Maine
Frederic Gardiner (1822–1889). The 1888 date is incorrect.

in 1897 and Elizabeth Hall of Brooklyn joined the following year. During this period women were only beginning to enter graduate and theological schools, and consequently few were trained as biblical scholars. Most of those who were so trained found employment in women's colleges.[9]

The passing of Philip Schaff in 1893 was mourned by innumerable people, especially his colleagues in the Society, among whom he was known as a prolific writer, a devoted scholar and teacher, and a founding member. The memorial resolution adopted at the twenty-seventh meeting in 1894 concluded: "We make grateful mention, also, of the kind offices of Dr. Schaff, at the very inception of the Society. His name stands on the first page of our book of records,—the first name found there; and we shall always hold it in affectionate remembrance" (13 [1894] iv). The great Swiss scholar was one of a remarkable succession whose migrations to North America have profoundly influenced and enriched the social and scholarly life of the Society.

Programs and Structure

From the outset, the structure of the Society was flexible and functional, reflecting the changing interests and moods of the members—at least if the frequent alterations of the constitution may be taken as a sign. Within the first decade, revisions were made in no fewer than five meetings. At the twelfth meeting in 1885, the growing tasks of record keeping prompted a decision to allocate fifty dollars annually "to be paid to the Secretary and the same amount to the Treasurer." But the action was rescinded abruptly four years later with explanation left to the fancies of future readers of the *Journal*. (However, the two secretaries were reimbursed for travel expenses.) The first printed treasurer's report listed a cash balance of $281.12 on hand 2 June 1887 and liabilities of $302.80; thus did the Society share the plight of most academic associations. Intellectual stimulation is seldom accompanied by fiscal solvency.

After analyzing the content of the first ten years of the *JBL*, Thomas H. Olbricht observed that the principal focus of the articles was philological study. One notes also, however, text critical contributions such as those of Abbot and Dwight, briefings about new manuscripts by Isaac H. Hall and J. Rendel Harris, and some interest in the newest investigative discipline applied to the study of antiquity, namely, archaeology. From 1882 on a place was reserved in the program for brief notes on particular texts and reports of recent significant literature and research, and archaeological matters were often taken up in this period. In the twelfth meeting in 1885 William H. Ward reported on the American Oriental Society's "Wolfe Expedition," which had surveyed sites in Marash, Mosul, Khorsabad,

---

[9] See further Dorothy C. Bass, "Women's Studies and Biblical Studies: An Historical Perspective," *Journal for the Study of the Old Testament* 22 (1982) 6–12.

Nemrûd, Baghdad in southern Babylonia, studying and photographing bas-reliefs, inscriptions, friezes, colossal lions, and altars. The expedition was endorsed officially by the Society at that meeting. At the fourteenth meeting in 1887 Francis Brown read a paper entitled "Ur Kasdîm," discussing critical inquiries about the location.

Many of the papers disclose conservative to moderate positions with reference to critical study of the scriptures. Edwin C. Bissell concluded his paper, "The Independent Legislation of Deuteronomy," with this observation:

> The reasoning employed in this paper, to show the independent legislation of Deuter-onomy is Mosaic, bears with equal force against the theory that it has undergone any special revision, in a period subsequent to Moses. There is neither in form, spirit, or language, any valid evidence whatever of any such revision in the series of laws we have passed under review. (3 [1883] 89)

M. J. Cramer argued for the Pauline authorship of the Pastorals (7 [1887] 3–32) and Frederic Gardiner concluded that Matthew wrote the Logia in Aramaic, caused it to be translated into Greek, and added the narrative in Greek (9 [1890] 16). George A. Barton took a more cautious stand in his paper, "Ashteroth and Her Influence in the OT." He wrote: "The critical analysis of the OT is of too recent origin for its theories to have been proved or disproved to the satisfaction of all scholars. . . . The part of scholarship, as of faith, is to work and wait, to seek for fact, but not to dogmatize" (10 [1891] 73).

But other voices spoke too. C. A. Briggs dealt with the discriminating use of the argument *e silentio* (3 [1883] 3–21). Benjamin W. Bacon pub-lished the first part of a four-section study, "JE in the Middle Books of the Pentateuch" (9 [1890] 161–200). At the time he was in his second and last pastorate, but he was already an enthusiastic advocate of German Penta-teuchal criticism. His paper reveals his skill in utilizing the new approach to an understanding of the documents in their historical development, some-thing not found at Yale in his student days in the early eighties. The same volume of the *Journal* contains an article by George Foot Moore, "Tatian's Diatessaron and the Analysis of the Pentateuch," an ingenious comparison that strengthened the case for a documentary analysis. The overall position of the Society was impartial, it seems, providing a forum for the expression and critique of diverse positions on the study of the scriptures (see figure 3). Increasingly, however, the position of the so-called higher criticism won support. German scholarship, a factor in the training of many of the earliest members, inevitably prevailed, perhaps signaled by the earliest statement of purpose in the 1884 revision of the constitution: "The object of the Society shall be to stimulate the critical study of the Scriptures by presenting, dis-cussing, and publishing original papers on Biblical topics."

Some of these scholars published more controversial papers in contem-porary intellectual journals such as the *Andover Review*, the *Unitarian*

Society of Biblical Literature and Exegesis.

——————

NEWTON CENTRE, Mass., December 12, 1889.

DEAR SIR:

The meeting in Boston will be held at the Theological School of Boston University, 72 Mt. Vernon Street beginning on Thursday, December 26, at 7.30 p.m., and continuing through Friday afternoon.

The following papers will probably be presented:

Workman's Conspectus of the Variations between the Hebrew and Greek Jeremiah	Prof. H. P. SMITH
The Vocabulary of the Synoptic Gospels	Rev. EDWIN W. RICE
The Biblical Demonology	Prof. C. H. TOY
On a curious passage in Barnabas. An important New Testament Manuscript, allied to the Codex Sinaiticus	Prof. J. RENDEL HARRIS
The Ascension of Isaiah; a new translation with introduction and brief notes	Prof. G. H. SCHODDE
New Testament Terms descriptive of the Great Change	Prof. B. B. WARFIELD
Babylonian Cosmogonic Myths compared with the accounts of Creation in Genesis	Prof. D. G. LYON
A Review of the Syrian Witness to the Apocalypse as stated by Tischendorf and Tregelles	Prof. I. H. HALL
Some Notes on Hebrew Lexicography	Prof. FRANCIS BROWN
Analysis of the Plagues of Egypt	Prof. C. A. BRIGGS
Purgation versus Purgatory	Rev. J. W. HALEY
Exegesis of Isaiah 7: 10-17	Prof. C. R. BROWN
Tatian's Diatessaron and the Analysis of the Pentateuch	Prof. G. F. MOORE

Briefer notes and reviews will be presented by several members of the Society.

Yours truly,

CHARLES RUFUS BROWN,

Recording Secretary.

Figure 3. Announcement of the Nineteenth Meeting, 1889

Review, the *Presbyterian Quarterly*, the *Hebrew Student, Hebraica, Proceedings of the Society of Biblical Archaeology*, and *Bibliotheca Sacra*. George Day founded *Theological Eclectic*, which later merged with *Bibliotheca Sacra*, "to furnish the American clergy with selections from the best foreign periodical literature at the lowest possible cost." Gardiner and several others were involved in the Schaff project of translating and expanding the multivolume *Commentary on the Holy Scriptures: Critical, Doctrinal, and Homiletical* (1844–1859), edited by John Peter Lange, which for the first time utilized extensively readings from the newly discovered Codex Sinaiticus. Charles Short and twelve other members served on the American Committee for Revision of the American Version, led by Philip Schaff, which produced the Revised Version of the Bible with Apocrypha in 1895. The NT, which appeared in 1881, was greeted with a phenomenal public response. It has been estimated that almost three million copies of the Revised New Testament were sold in England and America in the first year of its publication. Scholarly interest in the revision is reflected in the critical notes read and published by the Society members (see 4 [1884], 5 [1885], 7 [1887]). A proposal to consider publishing an American Standard Edition of the Revised Bible by the Society was made by R. P. Stebbins, but nothing came of it.

Structural and program changes in the last years of the century affected the Society in several respects. The twenty-eighth meeting in 1894, held at the University of Pennsylvania, was the initial attempt of the Society to hold its meetings jointly with other societies dedicated to the humanities (see figure 4). Billed as a "Congress of American Philologists," the program provided for some common sessions involving the American Oriental Society, American Philological Association, Modern Language Association, American Dialect Society, Spelling Reform Association (!), and the Archaeological Institute of America. At one of the joint meetings addresses were given by Society members William H. Ward and Herman V. Hilprecht. It is interesting to note how often such joint meetings were held in the early years with opportunities for plenary sessions as well as divisional meetings. In 1900 the University of Pennsylvania again convened a "Congress of Philological and Archaeological Societies" made up of the same seven associations. In general meetings, papers were read by George Foot Moore and Paul Haupt, representing the Society. In 1912, 1915, 1917, and 1918, joint meetings were held with the Archaeological Institute of America and several other associations.

Later it would become a regular practice for the Society to meet in conjunction with its sibling societies, the National Association of Biblical Instructors (NABI, later AAR) and the American Schools of Oriental Research. Moreover, in its early years the Society valued highly the cultivation of other relationships in the sphere of the humanities. SBL membership in the American Council of Learned Societies began in 1929.

From 1897 on, semiannual meetings were abandoned for annual meetings. It was proving difficult to arrange double programs, and the costs of

JOINT MEETING

OF THE

AMERICAN ORIENTAL SOCIETY,

AMERICAN PHILOLOGICAL ASSOCIATION,

MODERN LANGUAGE ASSOCIATION OF AMERICA,

SOCIETY OF BIBLICAL LITERATURE AND EXEGESIS,

AMERICAN DIALECT SOCIETY,

SPELLING REFORM ASSOCIATION,

AND THE

ARCHÆOLOGICAL INSTITUTE OF AMERICA,

AT

THE UNIVERSITY OF PENNSYLVANIA,

PHILADELPHIA,

DECEMBER 27-29,

1894.

Figure 4. Announcement of the First Joint Meeting, 1894

travel and lodging, borne entirely by the individual members, restricted attendance. These practices, it must be remembered, obtained in the days before the greening of America and institutional support of scholars in return for some token form of program participation. But the record offers no rationale. It simply reports the Council's recommendation, with the consent of the meeting, to hold one session of the Society annually for two days at the Christmas holidays. The pattern was fixed until the reorganization of 1970.

The revised constitution of 1889 made provision for the establishment of regional groups of Society members, with the consent of the Council. At the twenty-second meeting in June 1891, it was announced that a Chicago Section, as these groups were to be called, had been recognized. For reasons undisclosed, the independent-minded Midwesterners voted a year and a half later to reorganize as a fully autonomous society for biblical research. Thus the Chicago Society of Biblical Research, which was to exert a leading influence on the American scene, came into being. Not until 1936 was an official Midwest Section of the SBL organized.

Archaeology

This period in the Society's history was marked by a major development with far-reaching consequences for its life and work. In view of what was happening in archaeological research—recall the work of C. Clermont-Ganneau, C. R. Conder and H. H. Kitchener, W. M. Flinders Petrie, F. J. Bliss and R. A. S. Macalister in the preliminary archaeological explorations in Palestine, concurrent with B. P. Grenfell and A. S. Hunt in Egypt—it was inevitable that the Society would soon become interested in the examination of the material culture of Palestine as well as the exegesis of texts. The initiative was provided by Joseph Henry Thayer's presidential address delivered at the twenty-ninth meeting at Hartford Theological Seminary 13 June 1895. Discussing the historical element in the NT, Thayer made a stirring appeal for the establishment of a School of Oriental Study and Research somewhere in Palestine modeled after the American School for Classical Studies in Athens. Acknowledging the earlier attempt to do something similar in Beirut and an earlier proposal of Henry H. W. Hulbert, Thayer put the question: "Shall the countrymen of Robinson and Thomson, Lynch and Merrill, Eli Smith and Van Dyck look on unconcerned? Shall a Society, organized for the express purpose of stimulating and diffusing a scholarly knowledge of the Sacred Word, remain seated with folded hands, taking no part or lot in the matter?" Calling for financial support by leading seminaries across the country, Thayer predicted that "for two thousand or twenty-five hundred dollars, annually, it is believed that modest but adequate accommodations for the School can be secured, and a suitable Director."

The impassioned appeal won enthusiastic approval by the delegation. A committee of twenty-nine was appointed to draft a plan for a School of

Oriental Study and Research "at Beirut or other convenient place in the Bible lands." The plan was then circulated among a number of theological and other institutions of learning. The response in August was encouraging and a year later a more detailed plan for the establishment had been prepared and was circulated more broadly. That plan, further refined, became the substance of the structural form for the new school. At the June meeting in 1896 the Society endorsed a series of resolutions that called for a resident director, one or more associate directors, and students who were seminary graduates selected on a competitive basis for a year's residence. The plan further called for a board of managers, consisting of five members of the Society and supervised by a board of councilors, fifty in number. It remained only to transform the concept into reality.[10] Fund raising began in earnest.

In 1898, the Society responded to a proposal by the Archaeological Institute of America to enter into an alliance that made the president of the Institute a member of the board of managers and the chairman of that board. Two years later enough support had been secured to begin operations. The constitution had been approved, and C. C. Torrey had accepted the post of resident director. The good offices of SBL member Selah Merrill, U.S. consul in Jerusalem at the time, had found space in the Grand New Hotel formerly occupied by representatives of the British Palestine Exploration Fund. Twenty institutions and thirteen individuals had pledged support and constituted the board of councilors. James B. Nies of Brooklyn was authorized to begin excavation of the ancient city of Samaria. He reported that except for Jerusalem, a small section of Tell el-Hesi, and "four 'unimportant' sites," scarcely anything had been done in excavating the biblical period in Palestine. He estimated that 95 percent of the work remained to be done. Strongly funded excavations could be mounted in a number of important sites. It was an auspicious way to enter a new century.[11]

Issues

The proceedings and transactions of any society are often bland and frequently boring to the reader in another age. They tell us much about what is of no importance to us and little of what is. The official records of our Society, let it be admitted, offer no exception to that observation. A form critical analysis of the genre discloses that it is singularly sterile in furnishing the reader with clues about the cultural context in which it originated. If it is precarious to reconstruct the concerns and activities of the early church by an analysis of the *Wundergeschichten* of the Gospels, it is no less impossible to understand the biblical-theological controversies of the years between 1870 and 1900 by

---

[10] See "Constitution of the American School for Oriental Study and Research in Palestine," 20 (1901) iv–vii, the legislative form of a series of resolutions ratified by the Society in 1896.

[11] A full account of the history of the ASOR has been prepared by Philip J. King of Boston College and is in press.

reading on, beside, and behind the lines of *Journal* articles and minutes of the time. Is this because the Society was made up primarily of moderates and fence-straddlers on the issues posed by the new criticism? Is the silence explainable in terms of a tolerance and mutual respect for differences among academics, whereas the struggle was to the knife between church and academy, even general public and academy? We must appeal to documents other than official papers to assess the nature of the controversy, gauge the bitter and angry feelings, probe the issues, sift the debris. Scholars like Charles A. Briggs, Henry Preserved Smith, Hinckley G. Mitchell, and Arthur C. McGiffert stride through the pages of the *Journal*, but there are few intimations of how they excited the attack of others, how they met it, and at what cost.

We have spoken earlier of the impact of European scientific naturalism upon American life in the late nineteenth century, threatening the humdrum normality of the ecclesiastical and the secular communities. The world was perceived in a new way in the post-Darwinian period; new technologies brought rapid growth and with it preoccupation with material standards of life. In biblical studies, the rigorous analysis of the Pentateuch not only offered a new understanding of the historical development of Israel and its life and literature; it also precipitated disturbing questions about the nature, function, and especially the authority of scripture. It was a crisis moment in the history of scholarship, and it was unclear to many whether it was in fact a moment of truth or a release of the mystery of lawlessness.

With some surprise we discover less familiar figures in the Society explaining and defending the new approach to the Bible in book, article, and address directed to their church bodies and the general public. Edward Y. Hincks, E. A. Washburn, Orello Cone, Frederic Gardiner, Nathaniel Schmidt and others welcomed higher criticism and shaped their research by it.[12] Some paid dearly for their acceptance of the Pentateuchal theories of Wellhausen, Kuenen, and William Robertson Smith. C. A. Briggs, H. P. Smith, and H. G. Mitchell were among them. Looking back in 1928, on the occasion of the death of Henry Preserved Smith, the Society could say, "They [Briggs and Smith] probably contributed more than any other single influence to the adoption by the great majority of our American Scholars of the historical method of research as applied to the study of the Scriptures" (47 [1929] iv).

In an inaugural lecture at Union in 1891 Briggs, loyal to the Westminster Confession but a stout advocate of higher criticism, contended that he was closer to the original Reformation faith than American Presbyterianism. For

---

[12] For example, Edward Y. Hincks, *Some Tendencies and Results of Recent NT Study* (1901); E. A. Washburn, "The Aim and Influence of Modern Biblical Criticism," *Princeton Review* (1879–80) 27–46; Orello Cone, *Gospel Criticism and Historical Christianity* (1891); Frederic Gardiner, "The Bearing of Recent Scientific Thought Upon Theology," *Bibliotheca Sacra* 35 (1878) 46–75; Nathaniel Schmidt, *Biblical Criticism and Theological Belief* (1897).

him the real barriers to the authority of the Bible were superstition, verbal
inspiration, and inerrancy. A year earlier he and Princeton's redoubtable
arch-conservative, Charles W. Hodge, had founded the *Presbyterian Review*
as a forum for discussion between old school and new school Presbyterianism. But a storm broke over Briggs's inaugural lecture. The General
Assembly vetoed his appointment. His young admirer and defender, Henry
Preserved Smith, came under attack on the charge of violating the doctrine
of inerrancy. At an ecclesiastical trial in November 1892, Smith was found
guilty of heresy. A gentle, refined, quiet man, he was deeply affected by the
decision and carried his disappointment and sorrow for the rest of his life.[13]
His friend, George Foot Moore, resigned from the Presbyterian Church in
protest. Briggs himself was pronounced guilty of heresy by the General
Assembly of 1893, but Union rescinded its agreement with the church and
gave Briggs full support.[14]

A few years later, Hinckley G. Mitchell, secretary of the Society from
1883 to 1889, published a book entitled *The World Before Abraham* (1901).
Convinced that it questioned the doctrine of verbal inspiration, the Board of
Bishops of the Methodist Episcopal Church refused to confirm his position at
Boston University.[15] Tufts University then offered him a teaching post,
which he gratefully accepted. These punitive measures have remained an
embarrassment to both denominations over the years. In each case it was a
man of faith who was intent on serving the church as well as enacting faithfully through teaching and research a resolute commitment to truth.

In expelling these scholars in the interest of safeguarding the "purity of the
many," the religious community only impoverished itself. Church or
synagogue must be held to account for disciplinary actions of this sort. It may
be, however, that the Society itself is also culpable for continuing to evade the
basic issue at stake in the whole controversy, namely, the question of the
authority of scripture. The Society is a pluralistic group, with some members
viewing themselves as investigative reporters endeavoring to reconstruct the
origin and growth of the complex and multiform literature that comprises the
Bible and to perceive its role in the communities that brought it to birth.
Others are prepared to assign a normative character to the understandings of
human life disclosed in these writings. But these divergent views have rarely
been permitted to come into dialogue within the program of the Society, no
doubt because it has been thought beneath academic dignity or a lapse into
dogmatic disputation. Questions vigorously examined and decently put to rest
continue to experience a resurrection from the dead. But there is no textual

[13] His moving recollections of those difficult days can be found in his book, *A Heretic's
Defense, a Footnote to History* (1926).
[14] See Carl E. Hatch, *The Charles A. Briggs Heresy Trial: Prologue to Twentieth-century
Liberal Protestantism* (New York: Exposition Press, 1969).
[15] His own reflections on the unhappy experience are in his book, *For the Benefit of My
Creditors* (1922).

analysis, let alone exegesis, without presuppositions and these as well as postsuppositions require rigorous scrutiny and criticism if work is to be done well.

II

THE WISDOM OF THE SCRIBE, 1900–1920

Setting

As a new century opened, the Society continued to conduct its business and discussions in the fashion of other professional academic coteries, while the world around was changing rapidly. On the political front, the nation surrendered its traditional continentalism and emerged with a new imperialism. The acquisition of vast new territories—Alaska, the Hawaiian Islands, Puerto Rico, and the Philippines—and intervention in the internal affairs of Cuba and Mexico confirmed that the young nation was an emerging world power. On the domestic front a second industrial revolution resulted in huge industrial expansions and the rise of a monied aristocracy against which the workers organized trade unions to assert and defend their rights. The old individualism was challenged as new collectivisms emerged in the form of the unions and the women's movement.

The beginning of the twentieth century was shadowed by the calamity of petty wars, a portent of what was soon to come. It was a period when old political foundations were shaken. Europe was caught up in the midst of threats and rumors of war, which finally precipitated into dreadful reality, and soon the United States, Canada, and others were drawn into a worldwide conflict that shattered and remade national groupings and realigned the systems of political power. Academic institutions and their intellectual societies watched with shock the collapse of rationalistic liberalism with its optimistic doctrines of human nature and evolutionary progress. Enlightenment had to be reconceived.

It was a crisis in the history of civilization, to be followed by still more earth-shaking events in what turned out to be a war-ridden century for a civilization presumably come of age. The age of duchies and fiefs, pint-sized confederations and sovereign states, was coming to an end and no one was certain what would take its place.

Membership

At the thirty-seventh meeting in 1901, held at Columbia University, the program included the reading and discussion of seventeen papers. The first report, "The American School in Palestine," by the director, C. C. Torrey, appeared in the *American Journal of Archaeology*, Supplement to volume V. The school was secured by the support of twenty-one institutions. Martin A. Meyer of Hebrew Union College had the distinction of being the first full-time student. And the Society mourned the death a month earlier of the one who had set it all in motion, former president Joseph Henry Thayer.

Some notable names occur among those accepted into membership in the first decade of the new century: William Henry Paine Hatch, South Hartford, NY; Shirley Jackson Case, New Haven; Burton S. Easton, Nashotah Seminary; J. M. Powis Smith, University of Chicago. There were losses, too. The forty-second meeting in 1906 records the passing of William Rainey Harper, president of the University of Chicago, and notes his active participation in the Society from 1882 to his death. The memorial resolution spoke of the phenomenal success of Harper's enthusiasm for the dissemination of biblical learning among a wider public, particularly the fostering of language skills for reading the Hebrew Bible. He had promoted correspondence schools and summer schools for the study of Hebrew; the American Institute of Sacred Literature at one time served eight thousand students. The monthly bulletin, later a quarterly, *Hebraica*, extended instruction to over thirty thousand subscribers. Francis Brown, R. J. H. Gottheil, and H. P. Smith, who drafted the resolution, observed that Harper "had always taken a warm interest in its [the SBL] work, and had, in at least one crisis, done it a very special service." The "special service" (whatever it was) was gratefully acknowledged.

The year 1912 marked the passing of a man who had served the Society over many years. Numbered among the earliest members, Willis J. Beecher was elected secretary in 1884. He was still at it when he was named president in 1903—in all, nineteen years of service to the Society. Other founding members who had made major contributions to the Society passed from the ranks: Charles A. Briggs (president in 1890; editor of the International Critical Commentary and a leading interpreter of British and German scholarship, d. 1913), Francis Brown (president 1889, d. 1916), and Assyriologist William H. Ward (d. 1916). In the year the nation entered World War I came word of the death of Caspar R. Gregory, a member since 1885. American-born, a student of Charles W. Hodge of Princeton, he had made Germany his adopted country and was appointed professor at the University of Leipzig in 1889.

> On the breaking out of the present war, although a man of 68, he enlisted in the military service of the country of his adoption, and died in battle three years later, at the age of 71. He was the greatest contributor, among American born scholars, to the study of the New Testament Text. (37 [1918] iv)

This was a poignant statement of a friendship that refused to submit to the hatred fostered by two great countries officially at war. The ranks of the founding members were further thinned by the passing of Crawford H. Toy (d. 1919), Hinckley G. Mitchell (d. 1920), and Henry A. Buttz (d. 1920).

It is difficult for us to comprehend at this distance the fanatical repudiation of German culture and German people that developed in the United States during the war years: the boycott of German music and literature, the mindless hatred directed against thousands of German immigrants long settled in the New World. It was a sorry distortion generated by political enmity. It knew no social class but marked all levels of society, rich and poor, educated and uneducated. Yet the pages of the *Journal* reflect none of it.

On the eve of the war, the Society gathered for its forty-ninth meeting at the Jewish Theological Seminary in New York, heard addresses by two distinguished German scholars visiting North America: Ernst von Dobschütz and Arthur Ungnad. Von Dobschütz was one of three named honorary members that year; the others were Julius Wellhausen of Göttingen and Marie-Joseph Lagrange of Jerusalem. Wellhausen was then in his seventieth year; he died in the year the armistice brought an end to the hostilities. No mention is made of the armistice. Wellhausen's death is noted briefly in a memorial resolution that spoke of him as "the most brilliant OT scholar of his generation" (38 [1919] iii). In the next year the passing of Bernhard Weiss reminded American scholars "of the lasting obligations which our American scholarship is under to German scholarship and which the unhappy divisions of the past five years should not be permitted to efface" (39 [1920] ii). Occasionally brief reports were brought by eyewitnesses of the war as it affected Jerusalem.

The *Journal* continued to be printed in Germany through the period of the war by the firm of Haag-Drugulin in Leipzig. Early in the war the Council questioned this arrangement but no change was made. Delivery of the material became more and more difficult, however; volume 34 (1915) was long delayed. In the preliminary notice of the 1916 meeting, Secretary James A. Montgomery reported that "a few copies of volume 34 have made their way across the Atlantic, and it is hoped that in time all members will secure their copies." To speed the process the first two parts of volume 35 (1916) were printed in New Haven and distributed. Despite the inconvenience of long delays in the publication of volumes in the postwar years (not on schedule until 1923) and slow delivery, which taxed the apologetic skills of the editors, it was the decision of the Society by a referendum in 1920 to retain the Leipzig firm. The arrangement continued until 1934.

Programs

The first indication of a venture into the political sphere on the part of the Society is found in the forty-fourth meeting in 1909. A resolution was fired off to the Ways and Means Committee of Congress protesting the duty imposed upon books in English of a scientific and technical nature published abroad. It was argued that they should be treated no differently from foreign language books published abroad. With conscience aroused, they proceeded to join other learned societies in requesting the trustees of the Carnegie Institution of Washington to enlarge the number of their research grants in the fields of philology, archaeology, and ancient history.

War or no war, the Society gave expression to a developing self-consciousness and a manifest destiny. The fifty-first meeting in 1915 declared: "Although our meetings have always been held on the Atlantic slope, many of our members reside in the interior, and a few on the Pacific coast; it may fairly be claimed that American biblical scholarship as a whole is well represented within the ranks of the Society." Patronizing but affirmative! Perhaps Secretary William H. Cobb, retiring after twenty-five years of continuous service, had in mind the action of the Council at the forty-seventh meeting when it left the time and place of the next meeting with the Archaeological Institute of America to be arranged "provided the latter meeting is held not further west than Washington, D.C." Parochialism? Never. Well, hardly ever.

The earliest mention of an annual Conference of Biblical Instructors in American Colleges and Preparatory Schools[1] appears in the proceedings for 1915. This is the earliest form of the National Association of Biblical Instructors (NABI), rechristened the American Academy of Religion in 1963. Actually these conferences, held annually in conjunction with the annual meeting of the SBL, had begun in 1909 under the organizing leadership of Irving F. Wood of Smith College (SBL president in 1927) and Ismar J. Peritz of the University of Syracuse. Peritz was the first editor of the *Journal of Bible and Religion*, which began publication in 1932.

Throughout its history, the Association/Academy has been closely related to the SBL. The two groups have held joint annual meetings except for a brief period from 1966 to 1969. There has always been a substantial common membership in the two organizations, but members of the Academy have resented the haughty attitude sometimes manifested by the parent SBL in their relationships. Many members of the SBL tended to regard the Academy as a trade union (the earlier name suggested it) rather than as a bona fide research oriented assembly of scholars. With the transformation of the Association into an Academy and the widening of its scope of interest to include the total field of religious studies, its membership in the Council on the Study of Religion in 1970, and its recent (1979) acceptance into the august body of the American Council of Learned Societies, the old sensitivities and criticisms have begun to disappear. In a 1973 "state of the nation" assessment of major importance marking the completion of a six-year term as executive secretary, Robert W. Funk cited the reaffiliation of the AAR and SBL in 1970 on new terms as presaging a new era in biblical studies and envisioned "a new comity arrangement with AAR" to move together into a

[1] Also called the Conference of Biblical Instructors in American Colleges and Secondary Schools.

"study of religion in Western antiquity" that would not be limited to canonical literature (*Bulletin of the CSR* 4 [1973] 8–28). Today the two organizations appear to be reconceiving their roles in the study of religion as a humanistic enterprise legitimate in its own right.

From the fast-moving pen of Paul Haupt of the Johns Hopkins University (SBL president in 1906) came a steady stream of short notes that seasoned many an annual meeting and enlivened many a page of the *Journal*. Volume 36 alone contains sixteen notes; in all he published seventy-five! Each one was a substantial and scholarly study, though they often appeared under arresting and intriguing headings. Such titles as "Alcohol in the Bible," "Crystal-Gazing in the OT," "Dolly and Buck-Tub in Ezekiel," "Four Strutters," "Samson and the Ass's Jaw" are among the more colorful, teasing the imagination and inviting the passerby in for tea and talk.

Up to this point programs had assumed the form of a scholarly variety show, a series of solo performances interspersed with applause by the audience in the form of brief comments on the individual acts. Suddenly it was decided to venture some group acts—skits in show business parlance, symposiums in academic circles. A symposium arranged for the fifty-third meeting in 1917 was the first of its kind. "Critical Method in the Study of the OT" was the topic addressed by George A. Barton, Kemper Fullerton, C. C. Torrey, A. T. E. Olmstead and Julian Morgenstern. It was evidently a great success, for it was followed by a number of others in the ensuing years. A model was provided for other kinds of collaborative activity, and this has become the major part of programming style since 1970.[2]

Marginal financial solvency continued to be a problem. At the business meeting that same year Treasurer George Dahl announced that the Society would probably run into debt during the coming year. The Council was asked to consider ways and means of meeting the deficit. On motion it was voted that "the Recording Secretary [Henry J. Cadbury] should transfer his balance to the Treasurer." Was his modest pocket money sufficient to make the difference, we wonder? Evidently not, because in 1919 at the fifty-fifth meeting action was taken to raise the dues from three dollars to five dollars and to abolish the initiation fee. But the structure that had stood since 1880 remained intact, for a postcard balloting of the membership failed to support the action. The economic woes continued.

Archaeology

Occasionally during the war years word was brought about the situation the School faced in Jerusalem. At the fifty-third meeting in 1917, nine months after the United States had entered the war, Consul Glazebrook

---

[2] See Appendix III, Symposiums and Collaborative Research. Symposium themes are significant indicators of current interests and trends in scholarly research in the field.

described conditions in Jerusalem when he left not long before its capture by General Edmund Allenby. But the most encouraging word was an announcement that the widow of James B. Nies had made a gift of fifty thousand dollars for a new building that would serve as the permanent home of the School. In an amendment of the governance of the School in 1920 Warren J. Moulton became the first official SBL representative to serve on its executive committee in addition to those on the board of managers. Through this period, the annual meetings of the Society continued to be held jointly with the Archaeological Institute of America.

One of the unhappy situations that disturbed the fellowship for several years was the so-called Peters-Hilprecht controversy. John P. Peters (SBL president in 1900) had served as the director of the University of Pennsylvania's Babylonian expedition with Herman V. Hilprecht of the university's faculty as staff Assyriologist. Hilprecht succeeded to the leadership post in the fourth expedition (1898–1900), and from 1893 to 1910 he produced five volumes of cuneiform texts and inscriptions from the temple library at Nippur, a monumental and model achievement. In a paper read before the American Oriental Society in 1905 Peters, formerly professor of Hebrew at the University of Pennsylvania, made charges against Hilprecht concerning the methods of investigation related to the material from the temple library and called upon the university trustees to take appropriate action. In particular he contended that Hilprecht had inaccurately assigned nine representative objects to excavations under his direction of a particular section in the temple complex, described as the library, whereas in fact they had been found by previous excavators or dug up in other parts of the Nippur mound, thus bringing into question his whole account of the "library" find. Further discrepancies were identified in the estimate of the total number of tablets found and the number supposedly studied carefully. In reply, Hilprecht argued that the objects depicted were actually found in the library.

Though Peters called for a private investigation to avoid a scandal, the trustees published a committee report of a hearing held with Hilprecht and Peters. The findings supported Hilprecht but did not satisfy Peters and others who pressed the issue further. The Society was forced to respond to the situation when the *American Journal of Semitic Languages and Literatures* published a letter addressed to Hilprecht by sixteen American Orientalists (*AJSLL* 24/1 [1907] 22–24). In light of the charges, the Society at its forty-third meeting in 1907 declared that a complete reply should be made in the *Journal* or elsewhere. Hilprecht published a reply in the *Journal* (27 [1908] 93–98) and called upon the trustees of the university to permit him to publish all the evidence, correspondence, and documents. Permission was granted and in the following year Hilprecht presented his case in a book entitled *The So-Called Peters-Hilprecht Controversy.*[3] The proceedings for

---

[3] Peters's rejoinder to the book appeared in a privately printed pamphlet entitled *Hilprecht's Answer* (New York, 1908).

the December meeting of the Society in 1908 note that Corresponding Secretary Julius Bewer exhibited a copy of the book presented by the author. Nothing further is said in the Society's records. Presumably the whole unhappy affair was soon forgotten except by the principals, who must have borne its marks for years to come, though each continued to be held in high esteem by his colleagues.[4] This was something other than the sharp crossfire of scholarly debate over viewpoints that is the nature of theory testing in the academic forum. This was an academic heresy trial conducted in a public way and calculated to result in loss for both sides by raising questions about the integrity of the principals. We can only hope that the Society served a mediating and reconciling role between the two disaffected opponents.

Issues

The journals and meetings of most learned societies are crammed to overflowing with articles and addresses directed to fine, sometimes superfine, research activity in their respective fields of study. Occasionally someone stands back from these specific tasks to reflect on the total endeavor, the methods employed, and the areas calling for further exploration. A number of presidential papers in the SBL have been of this sort and offer valuable opportunities to the historian to take measure of the discipline in any particular period.

The 1889 constitution, developed in Frederic Gardiner's administration, first made provision for an annual paper by the incumbent president "or some other member appointed by the Council for the purpose," a tradition begun with Talbot W. Chambers in 1892 that has continued to the present time with few exceptions. It was the peroration to President Joseph Henry Thayer's address in 1895 on "The Historical Element in the NT" that galvanized the Society to action in establishing the School of Oriental Study and Research in Palestine. George Foot Moore has the distinction of being the only president who delivered two addresses, reading on "Jewish Historical Literature" at the thirty-fourth meeting in 1898 and "The Age of the Jewish Canon of Hagiographa" at the thirty-fifth meeting in 1899.

Francis Brown's address seems to be the earliest attempt to make an analytical survey of the discipline. At the thirty-first meeting in 1896 he addressed the twenty members present (an average attendance at the time) on the theme "OT Problems," in which he cited problems that confront scholars in the areas of text, literary criticism, historical criticism, and biblical theology and ethics. Sounding like a modern voice, he spoke of the subtle shading of textual issues into literary concerns: "It is not always possible to decide whether a particular case of criticism should be classed as transmissional or

---

[4] Neither the memorial resolution for Peters, who died in 1921, nor that for Hilprecht, who died in 1925, makes any reference to the painful incident.

redactional—whether we have to do, in certain cases, with copyists' weaknesses, or with the purposes of a literary workman." He deplored the use of archaeology as a conservative ally in the struggle of the new literary criticism, insisting that monuments no less than literary texts constitute historical evidence and as such require the same discrimination in treatment, critical evaluation, and adjustment to other evidence. He anticipated many of his late twentieth-century successors in his conviction that the great mass of OT literature dates from the exilic or postexilic period, and he called for careful study of the extensive editorial process through which most of the OT documents have passed. He concluded with the sage comment: "The vision of him who is willing to use both his eyes and understands what he sees, is a far different thing from the opinion derived from the imperfect and casual glance of even the most venerable among the Fathers." With total commitment to a vigorous scientific analysis of the ancient texts he expressed hope "that the members of this Society may do their full share in changing into exclamation marks of surprise and joy at real discovery those countless interrogation points that thrust themselves up from the pages of our Hebrew Bibles," a stirring commission to the scholarship of the upcoming century (15 [1896] 63–74).

It is a misfortune that the 1908 address of the gentle-spirited Frank Chamberlain Porter never was printed in the *Journal*, for "The Bearing of Historical Studies on the Religious Use of the Bible" spoke to an issue of scholarship and piety, reason and faith, that continues to demand a hearing.[5]

In 1903 President Benjamin W. Bacon chose to deal with "Ultimate Problems of Biblical Science." Lifelong champion of the European born and bred higher criticism over Fundamentalist "scribalism," this erudite Yale professor inveighed against a false understanding of Jesus' authority, contending that we must see "in the religious consciousness of Jesus of Nazareth the climax of the spiritual creation of God." Hence there is a need to determine historically the life and teaching of Jesus and to understand his God-consciousness, thus penetrating "more deeply into the supreme mystery of the spiritual evolution that is moving on around us." Behind ancient conceptions and expressions we may discern the essential truth of humanity in terms of its potential and future. The demythologization program was not to be defined for another half century, but Porter was arguing for an approach to biblical literature from a historical or developmental standpoint that reveals itself as a kind of "spiritual palaeontology." The proper purpose of all such study, he believed, is the understanding of what constitutes genuine humanness (22 [1903] 63–74).

---

[5] See the portrait drawn by SBL member R. A. Harrisville, *Frank Chamberlain Porter: Pioneer in American Biblical Interpretation* (Missoula: Scholars Press, 1976). The address was later published in *HTR* 2 (1909) 253–76.

President George A. Barton in his 1914 address, "The Hermeneutic Canon 'Interpret Historically' in the Light of Modern Research," continued his customary caution about higher criticism. He examined four branches of historical research that claim to decide disputed issues: source analysis, textual criticism, archaeology, and biblical theology. Assessing their contributions and pointing out their limitations, he concluded that the canon, used cautiously and continuously, can help set a text in its proper genetic relations and thus disclose its spirit and its effect (33 [1914] 56–77).

At the 1917 meeting Rabbi Morris Jastrow, Jr., called attention to "Constructive Elements in the Critical Study of the OT." He deplored the narrow analysis of documents that differentiated between the earliest form of a text and the glosses, expansions, and comments that develop from it. He argued for a larger utilization of tradition, reminding the critics that they must also account historically for the rise of traditional views even though they are rejected. Similarly, sociological analysis can provide a constructive element in critical study. The study of the development of popular customs and the tracing of their impact on Hebrew social institutions are necessary stages in the understanding of their literature (36 [1917] 1–30). The acuteness of his observations on the methodology of historical research is confirmed by current interests in tradition criticism and social environment criticism.

A year later, less than two months from the signing of the armistice that marked the termination of World War I, President James A. Montgomery made a searching analysis of the current situation in biblical studies in an address called "The Present Tasks of American Biblical Scholarship" (38 [1919] 1–14). Scorning what he termed "the apparent vanity of much of that in which we have been engaged" he scored the dilettantism of the professional scholar who has been exempted from the heavy duties other citizens have had to bear in a time of international crisis "because we have nothing to give." The great danger as he saw it was that in the aftermath of the war, many scholars would remain in their private paradise of scholarly research. "We think we are the heirs of an eternal possession abstracted from the vicissitudes of time," he observed. He charged the guild with evasion of responsibility in its failure to interpret the Bible to the public. Teachers must understand that the newest generation of seminary students would likely be more oriented to sociological rather than biblical studies. Our kind of historical scholarship was so confined to analysis that it had seldom contributed very much to the reconstruction of the total picture of biblical history and life. He made a ringing appeal for a new program of scholarship in America, which would develop its own resources and techniques rather than slavishly follow European, especially Germanic, models. Scholars needed research tools in English, financing for publication, learned reviews of learned books, major support for archaeological research, and substantial collections of manuscript facsimiles.

All in all, it was a rebuke and a summons to vigorous action and leadership in expanding knowledge and independent thinking that may well have startled many a listener. Few were prepared to pick up the challenge. For the most part research directions and methodologies continued to be set by European scholars once they returned to work. But the declaration of independence, motivated in part by a moral revulsion against the enemy and in part by a faith in the integrity of American scholarship, could not be finally silenced.

III

A TIME TO BUILD UP, 1920–1940

Setting

The interlude between the two global wars of the twentieth century was marked in the West by an unsteady economic recovery from World War I, followed by disastrous breakdowns, social unrest, and the rise of power-hungry nations which ultimately precipitated the second confrontation among the great powers. At home, in the midst of what appeared to be a stable and prosperous economy during the twenties, the nation was plunged into economic chaos commencing with the wild panic of the New York Stock Exchange in 1929 and lengthening into long years of acute economic depression. It is estimated that in 1933 some twelve million men and women were without employment. In that year, in an effort to stir the sluggish economy Congress passed the National Industrial Recovery Act. With new concern for social legislation that would offer some protection to a vulnerable citizenry, the Social Security Act was passed in 1935. Meanwhile ominous forces were mobilizing in Europe. In 1933 Adolf Hitler brought his minority group of National Socialists to a position of political supremacy in Germany. By the end of the period the storm had broken. Germany invaded Poland in 1939. With the beginning of German attacks on American shipping and the debacle of Pearl Harbor in 1941, the country was embroiled in an international conflict of global proportions that inevitably affected adversely its educational institutions and their ancillary research activities. It was announced in the *Journal* that Julius Bewer's contract to write a commentary on Ezekiel for the Göttingen series was cancelled "when the rising aversion to the OT in Germany in the thirties destroyed the market for such a commentary."

Biblical studies in the aftermath of the First World War did not succeed in striking out with the same free stride President Montgomery and others had requested. "We can no longer go to school to a nation against which we feel a moral aversion," he had declared in his presidential address in 1918. But German scholarship recovered in the years immediately after the war, and work on myths and legends initiated by Hermann Gunkel and refined by scholars like Rudolf Bultmann, Martin Dibelius and Karl Schmidt in what was termed (literary) form history was quickly recognized as a breakthrough to the preliterary traditions and processes of Israel and the early church. Vincent Taylor in England and Frederick C. Grant in the United States became influential interpreters of this newest methodological tool. The Teutonic *magisterium* triumphed over national defeat.

Judging from the themes of the symposiums and colloquiums, which became a feature of the annual programs of this period, interests were centered not only in form criticism but also in investigating and reconstructing the life settings of Judaism, early Christianity, and Hellenism.[1] The Society remained aloof from the issues dominating the larger religious and ecclesiastical scene of the era. The period from 1918 to 1931 was marked by major activities of religious conservatism in what is often called the Fundamentalist Controversy. It was the time of the ill-famed Scopes trial in Dayton, Tennessee, where William Jennings Bryan and Clarence Darrow argued the case of creationism versus Darwinian evolution as rival cosmogonies,[2] and of the enforcement wherever possible of ultraconservative creedal tests for clergy and faculty. Though members of the Society could not have escaped some of the effects of these tensions, no hint of it can be discerned in the pages of the programs and records of the Society. By and large the liberal position, represented by the majority of the members, was assumed without apology.

Programs and Membership

From the beginning, the Society members were interested in the textual traditions of OT and NT documents. Scholars like Isaac H. Hall and J. Rendel Harris reported to the meetings from time to time on codices whose clandestine travels had brought them to America. Papers on disputed readings were early offered for discussion.[3] In 1887, former president Daniel Raynes Goodwin reported that the latest count of uncial manuscripts of the NT numbered 91 (in 1972 there were 268). In 1919 the Society voted to publish a preliminary list of biblical manuscripts in America prepared by a special committee headed by Henry Preserved Smith. The results of a questionnaire were announced in 1921, identifying fifty Hebrew manuscripts, thirty-eight Latin, twenty-three Greek NT, eight Greek OT, seven Syriac, five Ethiopic, four Samaritan, six Aramaic, five Targums, five Arabic, one Coptic, and one Slavonic. An expanded descriptive catalog was published by H. P. Smith, "Biblical Manuscripts in America" (42 [1923] 239–50), an important inventory that was subsequently enlarged for the Greek NT by Kenneth W. Clark.[4]

---

[1] See Appendix III, Symposiums and Collaborative Research.

[2] Revived again in 1981 with the conservative theological (New Right) attack on science teaching in public school education.

[3] The first article published in volume 1 of the *Journal* in 1881 was Ezra Abbot's "On the Construction of Titus ii. 13," and the volume included a study, "On Romans ix. 5," by Timothy Dwight.

[4] *A Descriptive Catalogue of Greek NT Manuscripts in America* (Chicago: University of Chicago Press, 1937), now under revision and enlargement by John L. Sharpe III of Duke University.

The *Journal* notes the passing in 1921 of Professor George F. Wright, D.D., LL.D., F.G.S.A., surely one of the colorful figures of the period. For many years professor of New Testament language and learning at Oberlin, he enjoyed a reputation also as a scientist specializing in glacial geology. He brought Russian church music to the attention of American musicians. As editor of the influential journal of biblical scholarship, *Bibliotheca Sacra*, a post he held for thirty-seven years until his death in 1921, Wright had been an early interpreter of Charles Darwin for the American scholarly world and a firm believer in the fundamental partnership of science and religion in the joint pursuit of truth.

Other notable figures recognized in memorial resolutions were: William H. Cobb, librarian of the Congregational Library in Boston, who for twenty-four years (1892–1916) served as recording secretary for the Society; Ernest DeWitt Burton, a close friend and coworker of William Rainey Harper and president of the Society in 1919; Charles Foster Kent, who had made the results of historical-literary criticism available to a wider public in several series of college level textbooks; and Henry Preserved Smith. In the thirties the Society suffered the loss of stalwart leaders such as George Foot Moore, the first corresponding secretary and twice president of the Society; Benjamin W. Bacon; Max L. Margolis; J. M. Powis Smith; James Hardy Ropes; Arthur C. McGiffert; James H. Breasted; honorary member Karl Budde; David G. Lyon, a member since 1882; Richard J. H. Gottheil; honorary members Adolf Deissmann and Marie-Joseph Lagrange, to whom "more than to anyone else does the Catholic Church owe its successful transition from scholastic to modern scholarship in Biblical and related fields"; Nathaniel Schmidt, a member since 1888 and president of the Society in 1914; and Cyrus Adler, president of the Jewish Theological Seminary. All were leaders to be remembered with gratitude, whose labors long outlived them. Names of new members who would play significant roles in the life of the Society appear in the lists: Theodor H. Gaster, George E. Mendenhall, Harvey McArthur, Frank W. Beare, Mary Lucetta Mowry, J. Coert Rylaarsdam, Samuel L. Terrien, Robert Morton Smith.

These middle years were marked by a remarkable growth in size. During the twenties membership nearly doubled; by 1940 the secretary reported that there were 592 active members, partly the result of a vigorous membership drive undertaken by Secretary John W. Flight in 1937. It proved no longer possible to meet in plenary sessions in a two-day period. By 1927 the program structure provided for separate sections for OT and NT papers with a few plenary assemblies. Ten years later, with a full program of forty-seven papers, the annual meeting had been extended to three days. Moreover, in its forty-fourth year, 1924, the members threw discretion and tradition to the winds and headed across the Alleghenies to Chicago to hold the sixtieth meeting. Can it be doubted that a new and venturesome spirit was at work?

New guidelines had to be established for the presentation of papers. It was no longer sufficient for the presiding officer to suggest that a twenty-minute period should be adequate for even the most momentous discovery. At the 1929 meeting it was decided to require the submission in advance of abstracts not to exceed one hundred words and to circulate them among members intending to attend the meeting. Papers could be presented in any one of three forms: by summary oral presentation; by reading in full, if necessary; or by title, "whenever the subject matter is such that it cannot be easily followed in oral presentation, or whenever the member cannot be present in person, or when the paper can be brought adequately to the attention of members merely by publication in the *Journal*"—canny wisdom, more likely a guide than a mandate, unfortunately.

Further evidence of growth was the establishment of a Midwestern Section in 1936 with an initial membership of 262. The present network of regional groups dates from this time.[5]

Financial anxieties began to plague the leaders, a reflection of the national economic disorder in the early thirties, and attempts to cope with the shortage of funds were fruitless. In a surprising lack of business acumen those who attended the seventieth meeting in 1934 decided to request voluntary contributions of two dollars or one dollar in addition to the annual dues for that year. When no windfall of dollar bills arrived they heard editor Erwin R. Goodenough in 1937 tell them bluntly that they must raise more money or cut the *Journal*. Still timid, they decided to try voluntary gifts for another year. A year later Goodenough told them in desperation: "If the *Journal* is not now intrinsically worth more than three dollars, the Society should get an Editor who can make it worth more to them." That may have disarmed the last or next-to-last penny pincher in the group. They rose to meet the new demands upon them. Beginning in 1939, the annual dues were increased from three dollars to three dollars and fifty cents! The tide had turned. Let it be noted with awe that for fifty-seven years of it history, from 1880 to 1937, the Society maintained unchanged, though not unchallenged, a dues structure of three dollars annually, a remarkable act of fiscal management.

The semicentennial meeting in 1930 at Union Theological Seminary during the presidency of William F. Badè had been carefully planned by a committee chaired by James A. Montgomery. Even though the economy of the nation was in the doldrums, this occasion was celebrated with reflection, sharing of research projects, and congratulations from friends at home and abroad. The Society could take satisfaction in its strength of 448 members, 10 honorary members, and some 102 libraries and institutions listed among the subscribers to the *Journal*. The program included a symposium, "Palestinian Judaism in the First Century," and a record number of forty papers (see

[5] See chapter VI.

figure 5). By special action, the event was celebrated by the election of seven honorary members representative of British, French, and German scholarship.[6] The fellowship acknowledged with gratitude the life of Adolf von Harnack who had died in June at the age of eighty, an honorary member since 1904. At the anniversary banquet, greetings were brought from honorary and retired members Alfred Bertholet, Karl Budde, Gustaf Dalman, Ernst von Dobschütz, and George Foot Moore as well as from German and American learned societies and institutions. Former president Nathaniel Schmidt's valuable memoir of the history of the Society was later published in the *Journal* together with the proceedings and abstracts of papers presented at the first two meetings in 1880, previously available only in pamphlet form.

Reminiscences were shared by David G. Lyon, the oldest living member of the Society, who had been elected in 1882, Cyrus Adler, C. C. Torrey, and Henry J. Cadbury. One could wish that a summary on tape of those remarks had been made for future use! In his memoir of the history of the Society, Schmidt concluded with some forecasting. He reminded his listeners that "there is so much that of necessity is uncertain in our interpretation of the Jewish and Christian Scriptures," much remains to be done. He recommended the further development of symposiums on assigned topics of neglected areas of study to ensure more systematic and balanced treatment. Observing that papers had concentrated on the protocanonical literature, he pointed up the need for similar studies of the deuterocanonical and apocryphal books. He speculated about the establishment of a second meeting each year as an eastern and a western division with the whole group meeting annually in various parts of the country. One could no longer think of the Society as a regional club. The future looked promising.[7]

The 1934 meeting (seventieth) was a lively affair. Attention was focused on the well-known views of the Aramaic scholar Charles Cutler Torrey, remembered by a member as one who had "a Zeus-like appearance and spoke like an oracle." Torrey had recently published his book *The Four Gospels, A New Translation* (1933), which James A. Montgomery had made the subject of a sympathetic review essay.[8] Montgomery noted that the essay accompanying the "chaste and charming" rendition was the fruition of a number of scattered monographs and notes the Yale professor had produced over twenty years. He concluded that Torrey had proven his case for him. Torrey's arguments, linked with a combative style, forced NT scholars to deal seriously and competently with this revolutionary contribution to NT

---

[6] See Appendix II, Honorary Members.

[7] N. Schmidt, "The Society of Biblical Literature and Exegesis, 1880–1930," 50 (1931) xiv–xxiii; "Proceedings of the First Meeting," xxiv–xxxviii; "Proceedings of the Second Meeting," xxxix–xlix.

[8] "Torrey's Aramaic Gospels," 53 (1934) 79–99.

THE SOCIETY

OF BIBLICAL LITERATURE

AND EXEGESIS

TRANSACTIONS

AND MEMORABILIA

OF THE

FIFTIETH ANNIVERSARY MEETING

UNION

THEOLOGICAL SEMINARY

NEW YORK CITY

DECEMBER 1930

Figure 5. Program of the Fiftieth Anniversary, 1930

studies. And deal they did. At that meeting E. J. Goodspeed, H. J. Cadbury, and D. W. Riddle took up the challenge. For several years Torrey continued to enliven, if not polarize, the meetings: Hellenists and Hebraists of the primitive church *redivivi*. Some of the older members of the Society today can recall the supreme self-confidence of Torrey in debate: "If there is any one here who is competent to challenge these conclusions, let him speak. But I am sure there are none such here." Goodspeed charged that the maverick translation was in defiance of the scholarly ideal and "at variance with our whole New Testament science—textual, grammatical, literary and historical." As with the Paulinist's treatment of the sects in the Pastorals, argumentation was often by denunciation, entertaining but not overly instructive. Montgomery's plea for an unprejudiced discussion for the most part went unheeded.

The seventy-fourth meeting in 1938 was a joint session of the ASOR, the AIA, and the SBL, hosted by Union Theological Seminary in celebration of one hundred years of archaeology in Palestine and in recognition of the pioneer in the field, Edward Robinson. Several sessions were also held jointly with the Linguistic Society of America, meeting in the city at the same time. Papers commemorating the centennial of Robinson's first exploration in Palestine were presented by William F. Stinespring, Warren J. Moulton, Julius A. Bewer, Albrecht Alt, F. M. Abel, Millar Burrows, H. R. Willoughby, and Henri Seyrig, examining Robinson's contributions and reporting on current excavations.

Issues

The presidents of the Society during this twenty-year period occasionally reflected on the total task of the critical study of the scriptures. In 1923 Max L. Margolis continued to insist on the need for a self-sufficient American biblical science, calling for more collaborative enterprises of magnitude and less preoccupation with historical trivia. He cited such tasks as a critical edition of the Masoretic Text, a Greek-Semitic index, and the gathering of material for a study of the versions. His brief paper on "Our Own Future: A Forecast and a Programme" argued against an orthodoxy of criticism "hardened into a tradition and woefully lacking in self-criticism." By centering on critical analysis and genetic concerns as such rather than exegesis, scholars have failed to search out the developments in moral and theological thought in the OT which are integral to the historical process. "A presentation of the Old Testament religion which winds up with the skepticism of Koheleth fails signally in insight," he observed; a new sense of the worth and value of the scriptures for the life of synagogue and church needed to be rediscovered and shared (43 [1924] 1–8).

Biblical research—detached, rational investigation of the Bible and its people or historical scholarship in the service of the improvement of human life? The issues were brought into focus with penetrating clarity and balanced judgment in the presidential address of Henry J. Cadbury on "Motives of Biblical Scholarship," delivered in 1936 during a time of slow economic recovery from a period of depression at home and the rise of fascist aggression abroad. He reflected on the variety of motives that impel scholarly study of the scriptures, acknowledging that some continued to believe in the individual writings as the embodiment of revelation while others could not, though there was a fairly common conviction "that in the end some remote spiritual utility will accrue from the minutest contribution to truth." The tension, even conflict, between the two aims—scientific and apologetic—must be admitted.

In his own deft way Cadbury cleverly identified three sins besetting the scholar: (1) a preoccupation with anything new, (2) a modernizing of biblical situations out of a desire to demonstrate some practical utility to our work, and (3) the converse of (1), a hesitance to move out to new positions. "The history of biblical scholarship is marred by the too fond clinging to the debris of exploded theories." He concluded that responsible scholarship can never be divorced from the values, problems, and need of the hour. A responsibility must be accepted "for constructive forces that would counterweigh any destructive, unspiritual results of our labors." He cited a statement of the Minister of Science and Education on the occasion of the five hundred fiftieth anniversary of the University of Heidelberg, who declared in effect that the academic enterprise must be carried on under the suzerainty of the state it serves. This prostitution of the ideal of free scholarship to the level of partisan propaganda, he pointed out, may be contrasted with the mounting concern among British and American scientists for the social consequences of their laboratory work. The biblical scholar, he averred,

> may be in his processes faithful to the cold standards of history and literary criticism, he must not be indifferent to moral and spiritual values and needs in contemporary life. . . . Fidelity to the best in our professional tradition, both of piety and open-minded, honest quest for the truth, may prove in the end one of the most satisfying motives for us all. (56 [1937] 1–16)

In his presidential address of 1939 William Foxwell Albright reflected on the varied philosophical presuppositions that determined past and present attempts to write the history of OT religion. To his mind the most reasonable philosophy of history was one that was both evolutionary and organismic. Referring to the rejection of historicism and positivism by National Socialism he declared himself to be a resolute positivist. Despite criticism he reaffirmed his strong conviction that a practical monotheism appeared in the ancient Near East as early as the second millennium and distinguished Israel's religious thought at a very early time. "Only the most extreme criticism can see any appreciable difference between the God of Moses in JE and the God of Jeremiah, or between the God of Elijah and the God of Deutero-Isaiah," he argued, though not to everyone's persuasion.

Apart from Cadbury's comment about the Nazi subjugation of scholarship and Albright's strictures against an ideological approach to historical reality, there are no indications in the addresses of the catastrophe that was soon to engulf Europe a second time. Nor do the economic and social problems of American society in the aftermath of World War I find any explicit mention. Research activity remained in its own private world. More surprising, however, is the absence of any reaction to the sound and fury of the Fundamentalist Controversy of 1918–1931 and the threat to academic freedom posed by the ultraconservative effort to impose creedal loyalty oaths upon clergy and church-related schools. Obviously some of the members must have faced these pressures in their teaching situations. For the majority, no doubt, it was an intellectual rather than an existential issue. Secure in their understandings and supported by their faculties and administrations, they chose to devote their time to historical and literary problems.

These presidential papers reflect a variety of concerns about the motives, practices, and responsibilities of scholarly study of the scriptures. The refinement of critical procedures, warnings against a doctrinaire criticism, the struggle to establish the independence of American scholarship, the encouragement of team activity in the development of reference materials, and the tension between the pursuit of pure research and the acceptance of social consequences of the work—these were uppermost in their minds.

IV

SHAKING THE FOUNDATIONS, 1940–1967

Setting

In the quarter century that began with World War II the Society experienced extensive growth, set new research goals, experimented with new methodologies, and conducted a rigorous organizational self-study. There was increasing dissatisfaction among members of the Society with traditional procedures and a desire to move in the direction of a new understanding of research functions and ways to implement them more effectively. Changes were coming, in part prompted by dislocations forced by the war, in part imposed by an extraordinary increase of primary source materials requiring critical analysis, and in no small measure the outcome of a new interest in collaborative research work within the Society. By and large the program forms and the organizational structure had made few departures from the form fixed in the earliest period. It was essentially an east coast establishment based in New York City consisting of a small staff of officers and a regional attendance at the meetings. Members convened in a forum style to present the results of solo research projects and to enjoy a pleasant comradeship on a first-name basis. In substance it was an amplified faculty club, benevolently presided over by a cadre of senior and highly respected scholars who enjoyed proprietary rights among awed but ambitious junior colleagues.

Change was inevitable. The significant fact of physical growth alone dictated that. At the one hundredth meeting in 1964, an occasion of special celebration, 891 persons attended out of a total membership that had risen to 2,185. By the end of the decade it would be impossible to have the assembly any longer on a campus; only convention hotels would be adequate. The odeon gave way to the amphitheater, what one sadly termed "gala holiday conventions of colossal proportions." With it went a decline of the club atmosphere where each knew the other on a personal basis. But other factors entered into the situation of change. Much of the membership growth was occasioned by the entrance of hundreds of younger teachers, men and women, into the ranks. The Supreme Court decisions of 1948 and 1952 that dealt with the issue of religious instruction in the public school system were interpreted not to proscribe the inclusion of religious studies as a component of liberal arts programs of state-supported higher education. The result was a rapid development of departments of religious studies in these schools and consequently a wide range of job opportunities. Making their way into their professional associations this group helped create a climate for change. An intellectual aristocracy was to give way gradually to a democratic association whose leadership on the organizational level and in research and reporting would be more broadly based.

It was a turbulent period internationally. The United States was involved from 1941 to 1945 in a war of global dimension locked in combat with Germany for the second time within a half century and with Japan. This was soon followed by a controversial intervention in two other countries of the Orient—Korea and Vietnam, the latter widening to include other parts of Indochina. The Society records are silent about these hostilities, but we hear of a "national emergency situation" in the 1942 meeting. A year later, reduced attendance at the seventy-ninth meeting was attributed to a "current epidemic of illness" and some members "entering the Services of the United Nations," a coalition of agreements reached in the nations with common war aims and purposes which was an outgrowth of the Atlantic Charter.

A deep concern for the desperate needs of the families of German professors prompted E. G. Kraeling to serve as a clearing agent for American scholars anxious to help. About sixty people responded to an invitation and were matched up with a list of German professors. CARE packages were sent monthly for three years until the Committee on Aid to German Scholars was disbanded, a response of compassion that contrasted with the vindictive note sounded in the Society's declarations at the end of the First War. Strangest of all is the silence of a society of Christian and Jewish scholars in the face of the horror of the Holocaust and the absence of any public act of support for the European Jewish community or outrage at this act of genocide.

In the two decades that followed new and powerful forces were at work that reshaped geopolitical and social alignments around the world. The United Nations assumed a permanent organizational form and universal recognition as a necessary instrument of world order. Old colonialisms began to come apart; a new consciousness of young developing nations emerged as the Third World. A formidable bloc of Eastern nations committed to Marxist socialism brought about an East-West contest of political power popularly termed a "cold war." In support of the newly established United Nations Educational, Scientific and Cultural Organization (UNESCO) agency, the Society in 1960 unanimously urged congressional ratification of a UNESCO agreement on the importation of educational, scientific, and cultural materials. At home, the nation, uncertain about our involvement in the Korean crisis, was further polarized by our intervention in Indochina. The Council and the Society adopted a resolution in 1967 calling on the National Security

Council to reconsider its policy of deferring from military service certain groups of graduate students while not exempting others.

An explosive awakening of the self-consciousness of the Black population with a demand for full civil and human rights was accompanied by turmoil on the campuses of the country as frustrated and angry students protested our national foreign policy and the indifference to human needs and environmental concerns by a society preoccupied, as they saw it, with the gross national product. Women organized to challenge the limitations of traditional female and male roles in social and religious life. It was a world and a society in deep disturbance, the full effects of which can even now be only dimly apprehended. Something of that restlessness of spirit and search for a more truly democratic society may have made an impact upon the Society. Within this period the first serious self-study was undertaken and the first steps ventured to what proved to be a major reorganization and redirection of activity. The changes had their defenders and their detractors, as might be expected. To some it was a rebellion of youthful enthusiasts against their mentors; to others, a matter of making the Society the instrument of the whole membership.

New Manuscript Discoveries

A major stimulant to research that was to open new ways of understanding the ancient Near East and the Greco-Roman world was the discovery of new documents, some containing texts previously unknown, and fresh evidence of material culture. The twentieth century has been the beneficiary of rich finds from ancient civilizations more than any previous century. The first gifts had come in the 1870s with the discovery by Egyptian peasants of thousands of papyri in the province of Fayum.[1] In the late 1890s and in the early years of the new century, the systematic work of Flinders Petrie, Grenfell, and Hunt had increased enormously that hoard. Some contained biblical texts. The Nash papyrus fragments of the Deuteronomic decalogue were announced in 1903. The thirties brought to the attention of the scholarly world the important collection of eleven papyrus codices of the biblical books and some apocryphal material acquired by Sir Alfred Chester Beatty of London in 1931 and the fragment of an apocryphal Gospel bought by the British Museum in 1934 (Egerton Pap. 2).

But these were dwarfed by a series of spectacular finds commencing with the discovery early in 1947 of seven parchment scrolls in a cave near Qumran in the Judean desert, followed by successive yields from other caves at Qumran, Murabba'at, Nahal Hever, the chamber of an old monastery at Hirbet Mird, and excavations at Masada in 1964–1965. About a year before

---

[1] As early as 1778, however, natives in the province of Fayum had unearthed papyrus rolls and fragments.

the discovery of the first Dead Sea Scrolls, fellahin digging for fertilizer near Nag Hammadi in Lower Egypt unearthed the first of eleven leather-bound papyrus codices, the remnants of an early Christian Gnostic library. A few years later in 1954 appeared the first in a long series of publications of a collection of papyrus codices purchased about 1950 in Cairo by a Swiss bibliophile, M. Martin Bodmer. The Bodmer collection, rivaled only by the Beatty collection, contained extensive fragments of biblical and early Christian texts written in Greek and Coptic, the oldest dating from the late second or early third century. James M. Robinson has recently speculated that the Bodmer material may have come from a neighboring town to Nag Hammadi. To the scholar and thesis-hungry graduate student of biblical studies it was manna from heaven in unbelievable supply.

The first discussion of the Qumran documents by the Society occurred at the eighty-fourth meeting in 1948 when Millar Burrows, William H. Brownlee, and John C. Trever participated in a panel presentation of "The Jerusalem Hebrew Scrolls." Burrows, Brownlee, S. E. Johnson, and W. L. Reed constituted a panel in 1954, discussing "The Dead Sea Scrolls and the NT." Three papers on the theme "Recent Developments in the Study of the Text of the Bible" read by Bruce M. Metzger, Patrick W. Skehan, and Harry M. Orlinsky before the American Textual Criticism Seminar in 1958 reported on recent discoveries of manuscripts of the Bible and offered preliminary estimates of the impact of the Qumran documents on the study of the Masoretic and Septuagint texts of the OT (78 [1959] 13–33). From that day to this, the pages of the *Journal* have contained many valuable articles by prominent scholars in OT and NT studies who are members of the Society on the biblical, commentary, and sectarian literature of the ancient library of Qumran. The pluralistic character of pre-A.D. 70 Judaism has been opened up in a new and exciting way.

A combination of political events including the fall of the Faruk dynasty, the Suez crisis, and the Six-Day War conspired to withhold the complete contents of the Nag Hammadi library for a number of years until James M. Robinson, working through UNESCO, pronounced the password "Open Sesame." The establishment in 1970 of an International Committee for the Nag Hammadi Codices assured the scholarly world that in due course they would be available. By the end of the seventies the facsimile edition and the complete English edition had begun to appear. As Robinson put it, "a tidal wave is beginning to sweep over the well-worn ruts of scholarship, as new maps of early Judaism and Christianity begin to emerge."

As early as 1959 Robert M. Grant had addressed the Society in a presidential address on "Two Gnostic Gospels," a critical analysis of the Nag Hammadi Gospels of Thomas and Philip. Earlier, in 1954, Grant had read before the Society the first paper on the new Coptic manuscripts under the title, "New Gnostic Books." Despite the slowness in publication of the source materials, critical essays on selected documents continued to appear. Later, in the revised program structure in the seventies, a special section was devoted to the Nag Hammadi library.

The problem of access to historical materials was by no means restricted to these Egyptian codices. In 1960 Morton Smith, noting that scholars are often denied access to privately held collections of Greek manuscripts, received the approval of the Society for a resolution calling for the American Council of Learned Societies to bring to the attention of the Union Academique Internationale problems of access to some manuscript materials for historical study. It was at that meeting that a symposium consisting of Smith, Pierson Parker, and James A. Sanders discussed "A Letter Attributed to Clement of Alexandria and Containing Quotations from a Secret Gospel Attributed to St. Mark," a late manuscript found among the flyleaves of a seventeenth-century Dutch publication of the Letters of Ignatius which Smith had identified on a visit in 1958 to the Monastery of Mar Saba in the Judean desert. In this instance both study privileges and publication rights had been granted by friendly church authorities.

The services of professional scholars in evaluating the significance of newly discovered manuscripts and protecting the general public against extravagant claims can go unrewarded. A notorious case is that of the so-called Yonan Codex, named for its owner, Norman M. Yonan, and the Aramaic Bible Foundation, established to purchase the codex and promote the study of the Aramaic language. The codex, a manuscript of the Syriac NT, was reported to be "the oldest surviving complete NT written in Syriac-Aramaic, the language spoken by Jesus" by the *Washington Evening Star* for 25 March 1955. The Aramaic Bible Foundation was campaigning to raise 1.5 million dollars to purchase the codex from Yonan and present "Christendom's most precious possession" to the Library of Congress, after its triumphal tour by bus across the country. It was reported that an equivalent sum of money would be raised to make facsimile copies and translations available and to promote the study of the language of the codex by establishing chairs for the teaching of Aramaic and offering student scholarships. Bruce M. Metzger, who had examined the manuscript, was convinced that the text was the standard Peshitta Syriac version commonly held to be no older than the fifth century. He and other specialists in Syriac paleography assigned a seventh-century date to the codex itself. At the seventy-fifth meeting in 1955 a resolution drawn up by Metzger, W. F. Albright, and W. H. P. Hatch was adopted by the Society stating these conclusions and naming five thousand dollars as a fair estimate of value. With it the Society voted "to give publicity for the guidance of the general public."

Scholarly responsibilities discharged, the professors completed their program and returned home to their respective schools, pleased that newspaper publicity was given to their action. Within a few weeks, the newly elected president, J. Philip Hyatt, was notified that unless a retraction was made the Society would be sued for libel by the Foundation with damages set at one million dollars, two-thirds of the asking price! The world of politics and business had made an assault on the ivory tower of academe. Helpless before the threat of costly litigation, Hyatt held hurried consultation with his associates in Council. On legal advice, they agreed to write a conciliatory letter clarifying their position on the codex.[2] The foundation, in turn, desisted from the suit after assurances from the Society that no imputations of fraud were intended. Whereupon the plantiff announced to the press that the prestigious SBL had endorsed all the claims he was making for the Yonan Codex!

It was a sad affair that raised unanswered questions about the responsibilities and rights of academic specialists to give counsel on matters within the area of their competence to the general public, even when that professional judgment has not been sought. Unfortunately the Society did not confer at that time with the staff of the ACLS. Two years later SBL delegate Erwin R. Goodenough reported in response to questions raised by Hyatt that the Council was interested in the Society's stand, that it would be ready to help in any future difficulty, and that it had the services of several eminent lawyers who would have been delighted to defend the original statement without charge. But it was too late. The Yonan affair reminded an embarrassed Society that Paul's question, "Do you not know that the saints will judge the world?" is a not-yet-realized eschatology. For several years thereafter the apprehensive Society appointed a public relations officer to keep watch, but boredom brought a swift end to that arrangement.

Membership and Programs

Membership grew rapidly in the postwar period. In the forties and fifties it doubled in each decade. The same percentage of growth that had previously been spread over a thirty-year period occurred within a ten-year space. In the single year 1956 more than five hundred new members joined. By 1967 there were 2,488 regular members and 191 student members. There were heavy losses among the senior members. The memorial resolutions in the *Journal* pay tribute to some major figures in the history of American and international biblical scholarship: J. Rendel Harris, Kemper Fullerton, F. J. Foakes-Jackson, George A. Barton, George Adam Smith, James Moffatt, A. T. E. Olmstead, Frank Chamberlain Porter, Kirsopp Lake, who had served two terms as president, Warren J. Moulton, for twenty-five years the Society's delegate to ASOR, Shirley Jackson Case, Martin Dibelius, and James A. Montgomery. The fifties extended the list: Robert P. Blake, Burton S. Easton, Frederic G. Kenyon, Mary I. Hussey,

---

[2] This is a correction of the common view of a retraction by the Council, which I had published previously ("A Century of Service to American Biblical Scholarship," *Bulletin of the Council on the Study of Religion* 2 [1980] 2) in the light of information found in the private correspondence of Dr. Hyatt.

Julius A. Bewer, C. T. Craig, Louis Ginzberg, E. F. Scott, H. M. Goguel, C. C. Torrey, Ralph Marcus, Albrecht Alt, James E. Frame, Thomas Walter Manson, Chester C. McCown, and Robert H. Pfeiffer. The ranks appeared to be decimated. These men and women had shaped, directed, and given status to the discipline. They posed the questions, developed the research tools, served as the mentors for a generation of fledgling teachers and researchers, and advanced significantly the critical study of the scriptures. Their academic offspring rose up and called them blessed.

These are the years within the memory of many of the senior members of the Society today. Their recollections of these members and leaders, their quirks and capabilities, fill the pages of love letters to a learned society, which they were invited to draft. Letter after letter recites the list of redoubtable scholars like W. F. Albright, Julian Morgenstern, Erwin R. Goodenough, H. J. Cadbury, James Muilenburg, C. C. Torrey, F. C. Grant, W. H. P. Hatch, Edgar J. Goodspeed, Shirley Jackson Case, Benjamin W. Bacon, Warren J. Moulton, Julius A. Bewer, Max L. Margolis, J. M. Powis Smith, Nathaniel Schmidt, F. C. Porter, George Foot Moore, R. H. Pfeiffer, Samuel Sandmel, and Kenneth W. Clark. Of George Foot Moore it was said that in his fifties "he could repeat verbatim whole pages from the church fathers which he had not read since college days as a diversion with his roommate." Of Kirsopp Lake: "He read an untranslated Greek Father as readily as the evening paper." There were others besides C. C. Torrey who were monuments of self-assurance. Of Julian Morgenstern it was reported, "He would hold forth as though he was there when God spoke to Moses and Amos and the rest." One wrote, "No one could be more positive and assured in the knowledge and interpretation of the Bible in its archaeological settings, nor more ready to demolish an opposing view than Professor Albright. I remember asking him once what he thought of Goodenough's articles and he replied, 'Absolutely fantastic!'" He meant it in the dictionary sense. The art of dialectics took unforgettable form in the floor debates of George A. Barton and A. T. Clay, C. C. Torrey and E. J. Goodspeed and D. W. Riddle, W. A. Irwin and W. F. Albright, M. S. Enslin and K. Grobel—often generating as much heat as light.

Cadbury is frequently mentioned, a lifetime member of the Society who served it with consummate skill as secretary (1916–1933) and as president (1936), whose addresses about the Society on the occasion of the fiftieth year in 1930, the seventy-fifth year in 1955[3] and the hundredth meeting in 1964 were not published, unfortunately, to the disappointment of the historian and our common loss. Once, explaining that he was to go on leave for a season of work in Jerusalem, Cadbury observed that he would not undertake excavation, because, as he put it, "I cannot dig; to beg I am ashamed." But

---

[3] A cassette tape of this message is preserved in the Center for Biblical Research and Archives at Claremont.

there were experiences besides those of awe and intimidation in the presence of greatness. "We gathered as peers in the washrooms at morning when the sight of a famous figure uncombed, unshaven, sleepy-eyed, and in pyjamas, somehow increased our common humanity."

Let one more correspondent speak.

> We settled into our classroom seats, knowing that the crowded program, filling forenoon, afternoon, and evening would leave us stuffed in mind, in fact, numb at both ends. We marvelled at Moffatt's entrancing grace and encyclopedic range of information. My youthful enthusiasm for Moffatt abated somewhat when I told my gruff teacher, Ropes, I had just bought Moffatt's Commentary on Hebrews. Ropes sniffed a bit at its light weight. I checked Ropes' Commentary on James' five chapters. It was about 50 pages longer than Moffatt's on the 13 chapters of Hebrews. Torrey with calm assurance proclaimed Aramaic Gospels. With soft-spoken, masterly ease he set forth evidence on the blackboard to prove that an Aramaic original, "Whatsoever would spoil is salted," makes more sense than "Everyone shall be salted with fire" (Mk 9:49). We glued our ears to the rapid fire delivery of Bacon while he agglutinated the gospel records. We heard Barton in quiet, Quaker tones relate Arabia to the Bible or explore a biblical word through its relations to a dozen Oriental languages. We traversed the millenniums of Mesopotamian culture in the measured papers of Kramer or the sprightly accounts of Speiser. . . . Goodspeed, who Americanized the language of the NT and the Apostolic Fathers, forthrightly discussed a problem in historical criticism and allowed small space to opposing opinions. . . . Bewer united German and American scholarship as he heartily translated and interpreted a Hebrew prophet. Scott knew technical details of scholarship but his Scottish practicality selected popular language when he waded through the Synoptic problem.[4]

Two principal anniversary events became occasions for special programs of celebration: the diamond jubilee of 1955 and the hundredth meeting in 1964. The seventy-fifth anniversary, or what Cadbury mischievously dubbed the "semisesquicentennial," marked the ninety-first meeting of the Society. An unprecedented number of papers (forty-five) were presented, including contributions from W. F. Albright, Theophile J. Meek, M. S. Enslin, and F. C. Grant; a dinner featured William Henry Paine Hatch as master of ceremonies with remarks by Julian Morgenstern and Henry J. Cadbury. Greetings were brought by guest scholars Toshio Hirunuma of Japan, Athanasius Hastoupis of Greece, and Vincent Taylor of England. C. C. Torrey had been invited to reminisce about activities of the SBL and personal recollections of former members, but failing health made it impossible for him to accept. Torrey died before the next meeting.

A more ambitious program was planned to mark the one hundredth meeting of the Society in 1964 (for the first sixteen years meetings had been held semiannually). Twelve scholars were invited to present major lectures: James M. Robinson, "Kerygma and History in the NT"; Roland de Vaux, "Method in the Study of Early Hebrew History"; Johannes Munck, "Pauline Research Since Schweitzer"; Hans Conzelmann, "The First Christian

---

[4] See chapter IX for additional recollections.

Century"; Arvid S. Kapelrud, "The Role of the Cult in Israel"; Gilles Quispel, "Gnosticism and NT Writings"; James Muilenburg, "Prophecy and Apocalyptic"; Krister Stendahl, "Method in the Study of Biblical Theology"; Nelson Glueck, "Archaeology and the Future of Biblical Studies"; and "Textual Researches since Westcott and Hort" by Kurt Aland, Bruce M. Metzger, and Ernest Cadman Colwell. Through the diligent work of Secretary Kendrick Grobel and J. Philip Hyatt, these papers with responses were subsequently published in 1966 under the title *The Bible in Modern Scholarship, Papers Read at the 100th Meeting of the SBL*, edited by J. Philip Hyatt. A British edition was published by Lutterworth Press in 1968.

At a gala banquet attended by many of the 890 who came to Union for the festivities, President Douglas M. Knight of Duke University spoke on "Literature, Faith and the Bible." Henry J. Cadbury, who had previously delighted audiences with his wit at other commemorative occasions, entertained the guests with his "Ninety-nine Meetings of the SBL in Record or Recollection." What a regrettable loss to his posterity that he spoke only from notes, which were not preserved. All that survives is a notation in the volume of essays: "Henry J. Cadbury, a member since 1911 and Secretary for many years [1916–1933] spoke on the history of the Society, giving many delightful personal reminiscences." It is ironical that a Society that specializes in tradition and literary criticism has been negligent about the preservation of its own tradition and records.

The Society was at a high point of enthusiasm and effectiveness. Its partner organization, ASOR, was equally busy. In 1964 there were schools in Jerusalem and Baghdad and research was being carried on in Jordan, Iraq, and Turkey. Two months later, the Society was shocked by the sudden death of its secretary, Kendrick Grobel, who had been responsible in no small way for the success of the hundredth general meeting and the publication of the position papers. Elected in 1963, he was the first to hold the newly conceived office of executive secretary. It will be seen that Grobel played a significant part in the organizational changes of the Society that came to fruition in the late sixties. For the next few years there were several brief tenures of office. Richard Mead of Vanderbilt agreed to act as secretary *pro tempore* after Grobel's death. Lawrence Toombs, who followed, was forced to resign because of ill health, and Walter Harrelson, elected in 1966, relinquished the responsibility after one year in office. With the choice of Robert W. Funk in 1967, a long period of change and development affecting every aspect of the Society's life began.

Finances

Fiscal problems continued to make life difficult for the officers—and truly miserable for the editor of the *JBL*. In his 1953 report Editor Robert C. Dentan declared that the *Journal* faced a financial crisis. He recommended a return to a semiannual publication, omitting the book review section and the proceedings. He suggested that commercial advertising, if admitted to the *Journal*, could generate desperately needed income. Some indication of a pinched national economy affecting members is evident in a report from the Council a year later. In response to an appeal for funds a total of $131.90 was received! More drastic measures had to be taken. In 1959, after bitter discussion, dues were raised from $4.00 to $7.50. After 1960 the proceedings of the meetings and the memorial statements were no longer included in the *Journal*. From that point on members and historians have been forced to track down these fugitive pieces in a variety of ways.

A Challenge to Change

In the two decades following World War II, conceptions of how scholarly work on biblical literature ought best to be done underwent scrutiny and reformulation. As a result the way was prepared for the first drastic alterations in programming and organizational structure in the history of the Society. The need and impetus for change came in the form of a presidential message that is surely one of the most remarkable addresses in that entire series. It was delivered by Julian Morgenstern in 1941. Three weeks after the nation was rocked by the Pearl Harbor catastrophe, Morgenstern attacked the very foundations of the Society. He faulted a literary criticism that perpetuated outmoded conclusions and failed to understand the cultural, intellectual, and institutional ambience of documents. There was need, he said, to assimilate new evidence about the ancient Near East furnished by archaeological and folkloric research, and it must be done here in America—Canada and the United States. The present war augured the demise of biblical science in Germany (a premature verdict) and a decline in the extent and authority of Bible studies in Great Britain as well. The tragedy, he argued, was that the Society was largely oblivious to all this.

He recommended the establishment of committees on research and publication, membership and resources, and program. He satirized the traditional program and procedures as a congeries of unrelated papers, minimal discussion opportunities, geographical fixity of meeting place (New York), feeble social contacts and exchange of ideas, the whole resulting in an insignificant impact of biblical scholarship on its larger environment. He called for (1) an agency for the publication of scientific studies, especially monographs; (2) heightened interaction with ASOR and ACLS; (3) inauguration and coordination of important research projects requiring collaborative efforts of a body of scholars; (4) development of popular biblical studies for the stimulation of lay interest; (5) establishment at selected universities, seminaries, and the Jerusalem School of fellowships for graduate study to promote development of qualified young scholars. To accomplish this, he concluded, new structures would be necessary and the constitution would have to be revised. It was a blockbuster that exploded upon the "long leth-argy" and the "unchanging programs," which were described as "conven-tional and routine." Although the fist was gloved, it was a stiff blow that stung to action. Vulnerable to criticism as the Society was, this was a severe dressing down from a beloved and congenial friend that had nonetheless to be answered. From the vantage point of the present time one is struck by the correspondence between what President Morgenstern envisioned and what has become the familiar pattern of present-day goals and activities.

The Society responded swiftly, appointing at that same meeting a com-mittee on reorganization, with eleven members headed by Morgenstern, but the committee was slow in getting under way. Reconstituted in 1946, it settled down to work. A report was made in 1948 calling for standing com-mittees on membership, finance, program, and research projects, limiting the delegate to ACLS to a nonrenewable term of four years (the first two delegates served concurrently for eleven years), scheduling meetings outside the New York area once every four years. To legitimate these drastic pro-posals, a committee was raised to incorporate them into the constitution. A year later the Society adopted the new structure embodied in a revised con-stitution and set of by-laws. Something new was happening.

Self-examination persisted in other quarters. Editor Erwin R. Good-enough stirred up a hornet's nest at the seventy-eighth meeting in 1942 when he observed in his annual report on the *Journal*: "The NT Book Review Sec-tion is a serious problem. In this country and abroad NT scholarship has hit the nadir. Not at any time for a century and a half was so little of importance being written." He recommended that the scope of inquiry be widened to include studies in Judaism contemporary with the NT and studies in Greek, Hellenistic, and Roman religion and philosophy. Like Schmidt earlier, he felt the focus had been unjustifiably restricted to canonical literature.

Signs of Change

As a result of these calls to action, impetus was given to new research projects, publications, and program revision. After several earlier efforts by editors Carl Kraeling and Erwin Goodenough had failed for lack of financial underwriting, a monograph series was successfully launched in 1946 with the publication of C. C. Torrey's text of the *Lives of the Prophets*, a writing attributed to Epiphanius, with translation and notes. This initiated what has become a distinguished series of studies that numbered twenty-six in 1980, the centennial year, with the publication of D. L. Balch's *Let Wives Be Submissive: The Domestic Code in I Peter*.

Since 1936 regional groups had been organized to provide further opportunities for scholarly exchange and to open the possibility for a larger number of people to share the results of their work for critical appraisal by their colleagues. Catholic scholars and Evangelicals were actively involved in the regional groups before they became visible in the parent meetings. In 1946 there were three active groups: the Midwest, the Canadian, and the Pacific Sections (now termed Regions).[5]

A significant advance beyond the traditional individual scholar engaged in and reporting on research occurred in 1946 with the organization of the American Textual Criticism Seminar, a group research program. This was the first of what has turned out to be a number of joint efforts in dealing with historical and textual problems. Proposed in 1945 by Kenneth W. Clark as a special activity of the Society, the seminar was officially recognized as an adjunct of the Society at its 1949 meeting. The principal aim at the outset was to serve as a liaison between the Society and the International (British-American) Greek NT Project endorsed by the Society in 1948 as an attempt to establish a new and exhaustive critical apparatus for the Greek NT.[6] Members of the seminar have also contributed to a project of the United Bible Societies, originating in 1956, designed to develop a new critical edition of the Greek New Testament for translators and expositors.[7] Beyond these two projects, the seminar continues to meet annually with the parent Society presenting single and group studies covering the full range of New Testament textual criticism.[8] In the present program structure, it is designated as the New Testament Textual Criticism Section. The meetings of the section often continue the forum style of contributions within the general category of text criticism rather than a seminar format in which a specific problem is addressed by the participants.

Several innovations in the 1967 program must not pass unnoticed. For the first time in the Society's history the long-established threefold division into plenary sessions, OT sections, and NT sections was expanded to include a new section on American biblical scholarship. It was a harbinger of more extensive changes in the next decade. A committee of Council members led by Robert W. Funk and including Brevard S. Childs, Robert A. Kraft, and Norman E. Wagner was appointed to consider changes that might be made in the constitution and by-laws incorporating a revised dues structure.[9] When they finished their work that committee proposed sweeping changes that went far beyond the Morgenstern revision of 1941. In addition the

[5] See chapter VI.

[6] An executive committee and editorial board for the American committee to cooperate with the British committee was authorized by the seminar in 1948. At the outset it was anticipated that the Gospels would be completed within a decade. The task, however, proved more formidable than had been anticipated. To date, only the apparatus for the Gospel of Luke has been completed (1972) and is at the Oxford University Press. The project is presently sponsored by the Institute for Antiquity and Christianity in Claremont.

[7] Produced by the *Stiftung zur Förderung der neutestamentlichen Textforschung* of Münster, directed by Kurt Aland. See *The Greek New Testament* (United Bible Societies, 3d edition, 1975).

[8] See chapter VI.

[9] The committee was enlarged in 1968 to include W. Harrelson and B. W. Anderson.

Council heard a committee recommend the organization of a seminar on the Gospels "which will engage in a study of basic questions in Gospel research." Was such group research so unusual as to explain why the seminar was not proposed as a program unit? Instead the invited members would gather before or after the regular SBL meeting. Concerned about the Society's palpable indifference to some of the newer trends in biblical research, a smaller group of younger scholars including J. C. Beker, P. W. Meyer, Robert W. Funk, James M. Robinson, E. C. Hobbs, Helmut Koester, and Kendrick Grobel had begun discussions on hermeneutical issues in 1960 at the home of Hans Jonas. The meetings of this NT colloquium continued through the next decade until 1969 when they were merged into the Society program. Another spin-off was an independent biblical colloquium consisting of former Albright students who met during the time of the annual meetings. But there were dissenters. The Committee on Research Projects, established by the 1949 constitution, was almost abolished by the Council in 1966 but was then granted a stay of execution to develop research tools, identify frontier areas of study, assess doctoral dissertations, establish liaisons with publishers, and attempt to coordinate a computer-assisted research.

Even the form of organization went through a face-lifting operation. By action of the 1963 meeting the office of secretary was changed to executive secretary "to restore the traditional function of the Society secretary," they rationalized. The Council decided that the secretary must exert a more authoritative leadership in the affairs of the body on the analogy of the corresponding secretary of George Foot Moore's time. Among other things this meant that planning the programs of the annual meeting was in the hands of the secretary.

What's in a name? The 1962 meeting thought that it was not without significance. By majority consent an abbreviated form of the historical title was adopted; henceforth the organization would be known as the Society of Biblical Literature. A descendant organization followed suit a year later: the National Association of Biblical Instructors was christened the American Academy of Religion. Julian Morgenstern must have chuckled.

Issues

We may attempt an assessment of the issues of biblical research in this period by noting those addresses that dealt with the discipline and the directions in which it appeared to be moving. At the center was a rising concern about the dimensions of historical and philological criticism of biblical literature and the relevance, if any, of the postwar orthodox theologies for research. "Biblical Theology" became an emotion-laden term, eliciting either praise or condemnation. Morton S. Enslin's address in 1945 sounded the alarm. Addressing the theme "The Future of Biblical Studies" (65 [1946] 1–12), he deplored "the need of a new orthodoxy" and in passionate rhetoric vented his fear that, as in the German situation, we were "in danger of making research practical and serviceable to self-constituted leaders." What is called for, he argued, is a biblical research solely devoted to the discovery of "the facts" through rigorous, scientific, dispassionate investigation of the ancient literature. It was just that conviction that determined his editorial practices in the *Journal* over ten years of service, insisting repeatedly in his annual reports that the *Journal* would accept for publication only those articles that manifested "genuinely true, solid, unbiased, and responsible biblical criticism."

His position was echoed and amplified by others. Speaking on "The Current Plight of Biblical Scholarship" (75 [1956] 12–18) Chester C. McCown urged that if biblical scholarship was to retain its place among modern fields of research, "it must maintain full freedom of investigation, thought, and expression, with no claim to a preferred status or special immunities, and with no theological presuppositions." William A. Irwin, criticizing W. Eichrodt's "heilsgeschichtliche exegesis," declared that the sole task of the scholar was "to tell accurately and fully as possible just what happened, and what was understood about that happening and its meaning for man's life" (78 [1959] 1–12). Perhaps the most powerful defense of the role of the historical-critical method was put by Robert H. Pfeiffer in his address "Facts and Faith in Biblical History" (70 [1951] 1–14). Replying to Floyd V. Filson's paper of the previous year, he argued that the Bible itself presented several kinds of historiography, not simply so-called salvation history. He concluded that "the descriptive method of the history of religion on the one hand, and the normative method of theology are mutually exclusive."

Others were less certain that there was or ever could be an exegesis of a historical text immune to any philosophical or theological presuppositions. Nor were they willing to restrict the field of inquiry to canonical literature. The boldest statement was made by F. V. Filson, who insisted that every interpreter has an organizing principle, an interpreting platform or framework in which to assemble and order isolated items. For him "critical study [operates] in the life of faith and the vital role of faith [must be allowed] in the work of study and understanding" (69 [1950] 1–18). Amos N. Wilder challenged his colleagues to recognize that they needed to go behind philology to cultural anthropology and folklore if they were to understand the nature of mytho-poetic language in the Bible. It was quite impossible to reduce all biblical statements to discursive language expressive of historical facts (75 [1956] 1–11). We have already noted Goodenough's summons to widen the field of NT research to include the areas of Judaism, Greek, Hellenistic, and Roman religion and philosophy. Ten years later in his message on "The Inspiration of New Testament Research" Goodenough warned: "We cannot be alchemists, endlessly repeating the same experiments." The NT scholar must ask, first of all, about the world into which Christianity came. That required an intensive study of the thoughts, aspirations, symbolisms, and vocabularies of both pagans and Jews before and after the time of Jesus. Then the historical critic is in a proper position to examine the Christian documents and disclose in what their greatness consisted and still consists (71 [1952] 1–9). These issues find further expression in two program units of this period. A symposium in 1957 discussed "Problems in Biblical Hermeneutics," and the hundredth meeting in 1964 included among its ten chosen topics "Method in the Study of Biblical Theology."

For Leroy Waterman—concerned as Cadbury had been about the secular drift of society in the fifties with its idolizing of the natural sciences— biblical studies, while bound to scientific methods of inquiry, must not appear to be "antiquarian inquiries concerning our religious ancestry." Instead they must hold before a secular society and the religious bureaucracy the realities of human values and a determinative moral order in the world emerging from studies in the OT and NT (66 [1947] 1–14).

Reaffirmation of a scholarship devoted to the rigorous pursuit of truth appears in the context of searchings that include a widening of investigation into the social worlds of Israel and the early church, a recognition of language as a social and cultural phenomenon, and a persistent reminder that scholars must be conscious of the social and spiritual consequences of their work. The way was opening to more far-reaching revisions of the scholarly task and the manner in which it must be pursued.

V

A NEW THING, 1968–1980

Setting

Development and expansion in the midst of worldwide social and political changes mark the life of the Society in the last dozen years of its first century. The seventies witnessed spectacular achievements in scientific research and technology, attended by convulsions of revolutionary import in the social order. Astronauts walked on the moon, scientists sent expeditions without crews to survey Jupiter, engineered sophisticated computers to guide space ships, process words, and tally expenditures at check-out counters. At the outset of the period protest against the Vietnam War (1967–1975) that had succeeded the Korean conflict mobilized student and faculty strikes and demonstrations on campuses across the United States with sympathetic responses from Canadian schools. Students in undergraduate programs and seminaries grew scornful of historical studies in general and biblical studies in particular. The past had no place in an all-consuming present and a frightening future. Within a few years, an awkward disengagement of American troops began. Embittered and cynical veterans returned home to a humiliated society that did not know how to cope with a national defeat in a contest of arms.

The Supreme Court decision of 1954 in *Brown* v. *Board of Education of Topeka* and the Montgomery bus boycott sparked a civil rights movement known as the Black revolution. Among other things, it carried implications for the predominantly white membership of learned societies across the country. The entry of more women into traditionally male-dominated organizations and roles was also to have an impact on research and professional societies.

The arms race between the two superpowers, the United States and the Soviet Union, introduced the prospect of a nuclear apocalypse that caused Fundamentalists and atomic scientists alike to reconsider the endtime. Galloping inflation snuffed out the lives of many small colleges and their departments of religion, imperiled others, drove up registration and membership fees in scholarly societies, scared their treasurers, and raised serious questions about the viability of national AAR-SBL meetings now that attendance figures were rising above three thousand. By 1980, the membership of the Society had surpassed five thousand, but there was an uneasy feeling that runaway growth might result in a loss of identity and a secularization of purpose.

During the last years of the century a backlash of conservatism hit on many fronts. Fundamentalist Christians flexed their muscles in the political arena by unseating liberal politicians in local and national government and attacking public school . education for its alleged advocacy of "secular humanism." National budget cutting threatened the funding of many research organizations at a time when Congress had begun to support programs in the arts and humanities and the first federal funding had been awarded to research work of the Society. At the same time an Evangelical conservatism, both socially sensitive and scholarly in character, increasingly differentiated itself from any alliance with Fundamentalism and strengthened its presence in the Society. Theirs was a voice to be heard.

Turning Point, 1968–1971

We have heard the stern critique of the traditional form of the Society by President Morgenstern and his far-sighted recommendations for radical change in form and function that culminated in the constitutional statement in 1949. Morgenstern entertained a concept of a learned society that departed at many points from the models of the past. He wanted to turn it from a forum debating the results of the private research of a minority of established scholars into a center in which research was being carried on by a body of scholars. The provisions endorsed by the Society in the new constitution, however, were not sufficient for a growing number of members who believed the Society should be more actively engaged in commissioning and supporting projects enlisting the efforts of teams of scholars. Further, structural changes were called for, including limiting tenure in such positions as the editor of the *Journal*, seeking a new means of managing the monograph series, and stimulating new research activities.

The year 1968 at Berkeley was a turning point in the life of the Society. A year earlier a committee headed by Robert W. Funk had been appointed to consider some minor revisions in the constitution respecting a dues structure for life membership. On so modest an assignment the committee set to work. Before it reported the following year, a thorough revision of the organizational form had been drafted together with proposals that embodied many of the concerns about the way the Society could function as a stimulus, sponsor, and critic of collaborative scholarly activity. Robert Kraft and Funk were the principal architects of the revised contract. While there was resistance to radical change in the Council, it was not a standoff between the old guard and the young Turks, as they were dubbed. Had it not been for the support of members like Herbert G. May, Harry M. Orlinsky, and F. W. Beare, who recognized that change was necessary and inevitable, the revisions would never have been accomplished. The document approved by the Council in 1968 went through further amendment by the Council and the Society and was finally adopted at the Toronto meeting in 1969. Reform had been mandated.

In a valuable retrospective-prospective study drafted in 1973 at the completion of six years of service as executive secretary, Robert W. Funk noted some of the factors that precipitated the change. He paid homage to Kendrick Grobel, who gave expression to the concern, shared by many, that younger scholars needed to be encouraged to participate in the annual programs and in the leadership of the Society. The new constitution defined clearly an expanded base of participation. Growth in membership—in 1968 it had reached 2,718—required structural changes and a correlation with the growing strength of eight regional groupings. The activity of two working groups, the NT Colloquium that had been meeting for discussions on relevant issues since 1960 and the Seminar on the Gospels authorized by the Council in 1967 with an invited membership, furnished models of the working groups, sections, seminars, and consultations described in the new constitution. Increased revenues demanded for this kind of organized research would have to be provided by a new dues structure. In addition, Funk added, the development of the discipline called for placement services for young scholars, additional publications beyond the *Journal* and the monograph series, and the projection of study courses or institutes for clergy and interested lay persons. "We should, in my judgment," said Funk in his 1970 report, "give immediate and serious attention to ways of communicating with scholars in other disciplines, the Congress, and, of course, the general public." Many of these mandates to change were articulated by his experience through ACLS with what was happening in other professional societies.

Perhaps the most immediate and palpable evidence of change prescribed by the 1969 constitution was the program reorganization of the annual meetings. At the Toronto meeting of 1969—the first annual meeting convened outside of the United States, as Canadian president Frank Beare wryly observed—an unprecedented 115 items appeared on the program. The Seminar on the Gospels held its first session under the leadership of M. Jack Suggs; the Consultation on Scholarly Publications met with leader W. G. Doty; the Consultation on the Use of Computers in Biblical Studies with W. Murdock addressed new possibilities for computer-assisted research and teaching; and the first steps were taken for a Pseudepigrapha Project and an OT Text Criticism Seminar. Papers were classified into ten categories: Apocrypha and Pseudepigrapha, Biblical Archaeology, Nag Hammadi Library, OT and NT Theology, Hebrew and Greek Grammar, History of American Biblical Interpretation, Literary Criticism and Biblical Criticism, Eastern Mediterranean History and Religions, Textual Criticism, Septuagint and Cognate Studies. The program segments were chaired by persons not necessarily on the Program Committee.

Although not formalized until later, the structure of the annual meeting came to include six types of program units. (1) *Sections*, smaller groups more broadly focused on a special area, e.g., the Pauline epistles, appeared first in the 1970 meeting. They offer the opportunity for voluntary contributions. (2) Working sessions of *groups* are organized to explore new areas of research or methodologies in auxiliary disciplines or to engage in long-term study of one topic, e.g., the social world of ancient Israel. They feature prepared papers by a continuing constituency. (3) Members interested in pursuing intensive research over a five-year period may contract with the Research and Publications Committee to develop *seminars* for that purpose, e.g., the seminar on comparative midrash.[1] Seminar papers are published in advance of the annual meeting by invited members. (4) Explorations of an area of interest that might lead to a new *section, group,* or *seminar* take the form of *consultations.* (5) In addition the Program Committee arranges for *plenary sessions,* which feature guest lecturers and distinguished scholars in biblical studies and cognate fields. (6) Finally, the new program provided for occasional units jointly sponsored with the AAR. These activities offered opportunity for both private and group research, requiring active participation not only at the annual meetings but also in the period between these meetings. Satellite or cognate organizations with purposes commensurate with the SBL were recognized as Affiliated Organizations, holding meetings at the time of the annual meetings of the SBL and sharing in the general program, for example, the National Association of Professors of Hebrew.[2]

The trend was away from the forum concept to that of a research center directed toward reporting and publication for the wider scholarly community. Such a program diversification, centering on collaborative research activity while providing also for individual interests and private research, requires careful guidance. The total program is reviewed every two or three years by the Program Committee, the Research and Publications Committee, and the executive secretary to check on the progress of the work, assist in publication, and encourage research work in new areas.[3]

The Society in 1971 undertook a new responsibility, that of publisher, accepting the proposals first made by Secretary Funk.[4] With a mind to the need for small editions of scholarly works, plans were made to develop a dissertation series, text and translation series, and a series on American biblical

---

[1] The central importance of the revamped Committee on Research and Publications in the new organization was defined in James M. Robinson's announcement in the *CSR Bulletin* 1 (1970) 12–16. "It is the initial policy of the Committee to concentrate its activity upon long-range, basic team research which can be better organized through a learned society than through individual initiative alone."

[2] See chapter VI.

[3] The *Annual Meeting Abstracts* for 1973 contain, *inter alia,* a full account of the Annual Meeting Structure and Regulations, 77–91, reprinted in the *SBL Member's Handbook* (1980) 9–17.

[4] See chapter VII and R. W. Funk, "The Learned Society as Publisher and the University Press," *CSR Bulletin* 4 (1973) 3–13.

scholarship. Reference works were to be issued, out-of-print books repub-
lished, and cooperative publishing with commercial firms encouraged. First
ventures were the *Book of Abstracts with Reports* and the two-volume *Seminar Papers* for the 1971 meeting. Since that time, the trickle has swelled to
a torrent as the Society has set the pace for other professional guilds.

New situations were adding new duties to all the members, including
the president of the Society. The framers of the constitution were convinced
that this office should not be determined solely by outstanding scholarly
achievement but also by the capability for aggressive leadership in charting
the future of the Society and its programs. The creation of an office of honorary president in 1968 satisfied the need to offer homage to scholarly
accomplishment and to exercise protocol on court occasions. Harry M.
Orlinsky inaugurated the new breed of working presidents.

The years 1969 to 1971 were years of ferment and innovation, setting the
Society on a new course. There were grateful recognitions, too, of past
achievements and former glories. Retiring editor, Morton S. Enslin, was affectionately feted by his colleagues in 1969 for ten years of service in the publication of forty issues of the *Journal*. True to his strong conviction of the purpose
of the Society, he had encouraged articles on biblical scholarship within the
classical frame of philology, history, literature, and exegesis. A stubborn advocate of the philological and historical fields as the traditional and legitimate
terrain of research, his editorship marked the climax of the first era of the
Society. With sadness for some, satisfaction for others, the present moment
was a passage into a new period of the Society's history. V. M. Rogers, honored
in 1970 for fourteen years of faithful service as treasurer, must have gasped
along with many members at the overnight rise of dues from nine dollars to
fifteen dollars and the arrangements for automated bookkeeping services. The
years were gone when a few hundred teachers of scripture could meet
together on a small campus to argue fine points of interpretation and swap
stories. Membership now was pushing three thousand, augmented by nearly as
many AAR members. From Toronto on, hotels and convention centers alone
could accommodate the crowd. Frederic Gardiner's group meeting in E. A.
Washburn's study would have been flabbergasted.

On a still wider scale there was a developing awareness of the need to
coordinate the work of a number of organizations specializing in the scientific criticism of religious phenomena in human experience. In 1969 the
Society voted full participation in the newly constructed Council on the
Study of Religion, a federation of six (now fourteen) professional societies
"interested in developing greater coordination of the field as a whole."[5]

The confusion of events in Palestine since the War of Liberation (1948–
1949) began to settle into a new configuration after the Six-Day War of 1967

---

[5] The *CSR Bulletin* carries announcements and news of the SBL, occasional delegate reports,
and, most recently, the minutes of the annual meetings.

with important consequences for archaeological activity in the Holy Land. In the early seventies field activity had been severely restricted because of the political situation and a critical shortage of funds. But the tide was turning. At the Los Angeles congress, heartening news was heard of new financial support offered by the Smithsonian Institution, the National Endowment for the Humanities, and the Zion Foundation for research projects in biblical archaeology. In 1970 the Jerusalem School, now on Israeli-annexed territory, was renamed the W. F. Albright Institute of Archaeological Research. The American Center of Oriental Research in Amman (established 1971), and an Institute for Archaeological Research in Beirut and in Baghdad were mapping out work to be done. In itself this was a tribute and memorial to three outstanding archaeologists whose passing was mourned: William F. Albright, Roland de Vaux, and Nelson Glueck.

The International Congress of 1972

The long-time dream of a world congress of specialists in religious studies was realized in 1972 when the International Congress of Learned Societies in the Field of Religion assembled in Los Angeles, a major event in the history of research in religion. The scheme was first broached by President Kenneth W. Clark to the Council in 1965 and a committee was appointed to investigate the possibility of an "International Congress of Biblical Societies" at some future date. Planning began afresh in 1968. The concept was revised and expanded when the newly founded CSR undertook the sponsorship in 1969, appropriate to its purpose of facilitating cooperation among the member societies. Under the competent direction of James M. Robinson the Congress Planning Committee of twenty-two set to work to prepare for a mammoth assembly that would bring together scholars from all over the world to dialogue on the theme "Religion and the Humanizing of Man."[6] The Council had been successful in obtaining a grant of fifty thousand dollars from the ACLS with additional support from the School of Theology at Claremont and the Claremont Graduate School. Preparations were made to accommodate some three thousand delegates; the total attendance was 2,553 with 233 overseas participants.

The congress proved to be a precedent-setting event. In all, eighteen societies were represented along with some smaller satellite groups. Three European groups: the Society for NT Studies, the Society for OT Study, and the Societas Ethica; the NT Society of South Africa; the Northeast Asia Association of Theological Schools; the Japan Society of Christian Studies, and the Society for OT Studies in Japan—all sent delegations.[7] Steered skillfully

---

[6] The plenary addresses were subsequently published as *Religion and the Humanizing of Man* (ed. J. M. Robinson; CSR, 1972; 2d rev. ed., 1973).

[7] The serial Studies in the Religion of Ancient Israel (Leiden: Brill) was initiated by the editorial board of *Vetus Testamentum* in commemoration of the 1972 congress.

by Lane C. McGaughy, the congress heard prominent scholars and theologians address the issues of new tasks of ethics, Christian humanism, the Buddhist and Christian responses to human nature and the human predicament, the impact of the Holocaust, political theology, the ancient Greek tradition on humanization, and anthropomorphism and the humanity of God.

It was a full-scale attempt to coordinate the annual meetings of a variety of societies in the field and it afforded a unique opportunity for exchange between scholars of related disciplines coming from differing confessional backgrounds and cultures. To be sure, the congress was dominated by North Americans, but the stage had been set for future conclaves in which stronger representation from Central and South America, the Orient, and the Third World was hoped for. The academies of religion no less than the councils of churches and synagogues were yet to experience the cross-cultural debates and fellowship modeled in the political sphere by the United Nations. There was a world to be encountered beyond the Anglo-European coalition, and Los Angeles marked a milestone in the journey into it.

Rounding Out the Century

Meanwhile the Society was enjoying robust health. Membership had climbed to 2,966; within the new structure of the annual meetings there were thirty-seven seminars and sections actively at work. Indeed, outgoing secretary Funk confided to the Council that his office had become a full-time operation, relieved in some measure for his successor, George W. MacRae, by the transfer of some of the membership and business matters to the newly established center of the CSR in Waterloo, Ontario. Nevertheless, he estimated that it would remain a half-time responsibility. Limitless correspondence brought routine and novel requests. Once Funk received the following note in his mail. "Gentlemen: Our class is writing papers about several subjects. Mine is Jesus Christ. I would appreciate any information you might send. Sincerely, ———." In reply Funk sent a copy of Frederick C. Grant's article in the *Interpreter's Dictionary of the Bible*. Unfortunately most of the duties of the office were not that refreshing.

The six-year period of Robert W. Funk's leadership as executive secretary (1968–1973) inaugurated a new era in the history of the Society in which he played a decisive role. Without his imagination and engineering skills it might not have been brought off. A top-flight scholar whose publications testify to his competence, he possessed the twin gifts of an inspired imagination that dreams dreams and sees visions and technical skills that can convert these ephemera into structures. Few combine the two roles. But Funk is equally at home in the diverse worlds of poetics and practice, brain storms and balance sheets, the catholic world of scholarship and the particular discipline of Christian studies. As such he is a controversial figure, but no one would challenge his seminal influence in reshaping biblical studies in America in general or the guild of biblical scholars in particular.

At the Chicago meeting in 1973 President Harrelson enumerated the accomplishments:

> The reorganization of the Annual Meeting, the establishment of Seminars, the reduction of costs of publication of the *Journal*, the extraordinary expansion of the Society's program of publication, the articulation of the Society's work with that of the AAR, the formation of the Council on the Study of Religion, the strengthening of ties with the ACLS and with its other constituent members, the development of connections with federal funding agencies, the extraordinary management of the records and funds of the Society, the development of the Society's regional associations into a much stronger group of scholarly societies, the establishment of the Association of Regional Secretaries, the bargaining with hotels for good rates at annual meetings—these and many more accomplishments we owe to Bob Funk in very large measure. . . . He has set an example for all future Executive Secretaries which it is unfair even to mention to his successor.

Less conspicuous things were happening in those days of change and development which were nonetheless significant. At the Atlanta meeting of 1971, a Council of Fifty drawn from AAR and SBL held conversations in the homes of some fifty academic and religious leaders in the Black community of the city. A few years later (1979) a growing concern to encourage Black scholarship in religious studies led to the formation of a joint committee of the two societies on professional development and standards which, *inter alia*, would give close attention to the need for increasing Black and ethnic minority representation in the field of scripture studies.

That same meeting saw the organizational meeting of the Women's Caucus including members of the SBL. A year later, in Los Angeles, women were prepared to call for a number of changes in the Society: participation of women on the executive committee and the editorial board of the *Journal*; the anonymous submission of manuscripts for evaluation for one year as a way of testing publication by a wider group of authors; the establishment by the societies in the CSR coalition of an open job registry for the field of religious studies. At the business meeting that year, two women were elected Associates in Council; one was appointed to the executive committee and full endorsement was given to the three resolutions sponsored by the Women's Caucus. At San Francisco in 1977 both the AAR and SBL agreed that their influence should be brought to the support of the Equal Rights Amendment. "The Society goes on record as opposing meetings of the Society in states where the ERA has not yet been ratified with the exception of agreements already signed, until the constitutional status of the amendment has been resolved."

Publication Program

The publishing program of the Society continued to expand rapidly in the early seventies. By 1975 there were fifty-two volumes published in addition to the *Journal* and *Semeia*, the experimental journal launched in 1974 that was "devoted to the exploration of new and emergent areas and methods of biblical criticism." Looking toward the centenary anniversary event in 1980 a new series entitled Studies in American Biblical Scholarship had been commissioned by the Committee on the Centennial, headed by Gene M. Tucker. More were on the drawing board. The Center for Scholarly Publishing and Services, organized at the University of Montana in 1975, incorporating Scholars Press, undertook to handle all bookkeeping and membership services of the Society as well as for other sponsoring institutions.

In cooperation with the School of Theology at Claremont and the well-known Institute for Antiquity and Christianity, the Society established in that same year a Center for Biblical Research and Archives at Claremont. Pierson Parker was subsequently appointed the first archivist using facilities made available at the School of Theology for housing and classifying the collected materials.[8] New research opportunities were announced with the establishment of a fellowship program that would make possible the financial support of one or more members of the Society for full-time research at the Claremont Center. A. F. Campbell, J. T. Sanders, and W. A. Beardslee were appointed as the first fellows for 1976–77. The Society was fulfilling the pledge made in the restructuring of 1969 to raise additional revenue for the encouragement and support of individual as well as corporate research programs.

Concerned with reaching a wider public and extending the discipline, the AAR and the SBL announced in 1976 a visiting lecturer program for religious study "to introduce the study of religion into community colleges or other colleges or universities where it is not presently represented in curriculum offerings."

The Centennial Event

With the establishment of the Centennial Committee in 1972, planning for the forthcoming celebration went ahead with increasing momentum. From the outset it was firmly agreed that this was not to be a retrospective and self-justifying occasion but one that would review the past for the purposes of self-assessment and projecting the direction of biblical studies in the immediate future and the ways in which the Society should aid that research. There was a heightening consciousness that there were social consequences and responsibilities of research work that must be articulated and accepted. Birthday parties were scarcely congruent with academically oriented societies and irresponsible in a confused and turbulent age.

Rapid growth in membership and costs was posing monetary problems in securing suitable accommodations for the annual meeting. The joint attendance of three groups, SBL, AAR, and ASOR had reached 3,500 at the New

[8] See the *CSR Bulletin* 6 (1975) 15–16.

York meeting in 1979. With an inventory in excess of a quarter of a million dollars at Scholars Press and an annual budget in excess of $200,000, the Society had achieved an economic status comparable with an industry. The amazing thing, as Executive Secretary Paul J. Achtemeier put it, was that all these multiform activities were carried on by purely voluntary services, without any monetary compensation to the hard-working officers and committee chairpersons. There were problems, of course. Scholars Press was in an insecure financial position, gratefully receiving assistance from its sponsoring institutions and associations to meet its annual deficit. But federal funding was becoming a significant support for research enterprises. The National Endowment for the Humanities had granted $12,000 for the Genres of Religious Literature in Antiquity Project and a smaller grant went to the Septuagint Lexicon Project. A grant of $21,000 by the Lilly Endowment, Inc. and an NEH grant of $87,000 made possible the Centennial Publications Program series on the Bible in American Culture. The ASOR had benefited from private and federal assistance for its Jerusalem and Amman centers. And there was an encouraging initial response to a Support and Challenge Project designed by the executive committee to give new fiscal undergirding to the Society. The problem would be how to develop programs utilizing these gifts without assuming they were guaranteed to be renewable.

Eight years of work by the committee, captained by Gene M. Tucker and Douglas A. Knight, came to a climax in 1980 when the Society met with its partner organizations in Dallas for its centennial celebration with a record member attendance of 3,134. The program was structured around five principal themes: Approaches to the Bible through Language Analysis, Social Analysis, Questions of Meaning, History and Archaeology, and the History and Sociology of Biblical Scholarship. Addressing these and related issues was a panel of invited lecturers including Langdon Gilkey, Hayim Tadmor, Edmund Leach, Martin Marty, Hans Küng, Frank Moore Cross, Gillian Feeley-Harnik, and J. Hillis Miller.[9] Panels of members had been chosen by the committee to present papers on aspects of these five topics.

At the centennial banquet awards were presented to the following persons who had made distinguished contributions to the cause of biblical scholarship:

---

[9] The addresses will be published by the Society as *Humanizing America's Iconic Book: Society of Biblical Literature Centennial Addresses 1980* (ed. Gene M. Tucker and Douglas A. Knight). The Centennial Publications Program originally included two series: The Bible in American Culture, in six volumes, and Studies in American Biblical Scholarship, in twenty volumes (both series edited by Kent Harold Richards, Robert W. Funk, and Edwin S. Gaustad); and a history of the Society. The list of publications has since been divided into four subseries: The Bible in American Culture (ed. Edwin S. Gaustad and Walter Harrelson), Biblical Scholarship in North America (ed. Paul J. Achtemeier, Eldon Jay Epp, E. Brooks Holifield, Harry M. Orlinsky, and Kent Harold Richards), The Bible and Its Modern Interpreters (ed. Douglas A. Knight), and Biblical Scholarship in Confessional Perspectives (ed. Adela Yarbro Collins, George W. MacRae, and Gene M. Tucker).

Frank Moore Cross, John Knox, and Harry M. Orlinsky in the area of scholarship; Samuel L. Terrien and George W. MacRae in the area of scholarly teaching; Bruce Vawter and Joseph A. Fitzmyer for their work in editing; Robert W. Funk and James M. Robinson for their skills in statecraft; Bernhard W. Anderson and Raymond E. Brown for their contributions in sharing results with a wider audience; Thorkild Jacobsen and Morton Smith for their work in supporting fields.

Concern for extending the services of scholarship to laity and clergy gave rise to a two-day program of Scholars Press Associates, which featured lectures, mini-courses and discussions on Judaism, Bible, Eastern Religions, Ethics, and American Civil Religion. Several hundred associates and friends took advantage of this special program. In the midst of this ceremonial euphoria delegates were surprised and sobered by the announcement of a structural reorganization of Scholars Press and the resignation of its founder and chief officer, Robert W. Funk. Both Scholars Press and the Society in this first century had been led by this scholar-administrator into a new understanding of their natures and tasks and had been challenged to move in new directions. Funk would be remembered as one of the outstanding leaders in American biblical scholarship, a latter day Moses who perceived a promised land ahead of him and laid claim to it.

How did the centenary organization stand at this juncture in its history? The physical shape was impressive. From the primary meeting's membership of 35 it had grown to a strength of 4,936 members. It was mind-boggling to anticipate the future size if the 42 percent growth rate of the last five years continued. The Society had generated a vigorous program of activities: regional annual meetings and a large-scale national annual meeting. Publications included the *Journal*, a monograph series, *Semeia*, and Semeia Supplements (now called Semeia Studies), a dissertation series, Texts and Translations, Sources for Biblical Study, Septuagint and Cognate Studies, Masoretic Studies, Aramaic Studies, and a series of centennial publications.

Modified somewhat in the light of experience, the ten-year-old program structure with its sections, groups, seminars, and plenaries seemed to have won favor and held promise of a productive future. Beyond dispute, the highest percentage ever of the membership was actively at work within the Society with impressive results in their own academic development and the advancement of the discipline. Never before had so much been said by so many. This was not without some disadvantage, particularly in the area of quality control. Not only the stimulation of research activity but also the rigorous criticism of its progress and conclusions was essential. The future might well dictate the perfecting of more finely honed evaluative procedures.

There were twenty-three sections at work along with six seminars and fourteen groups. There were twelve regional groupings scattered across the country, each holding an annual meeting. The Society was in affiliate relationship with six other research groups devoted to similar programs of religious studies.[10] It held constituent membership in the ACLS and the CSR. Program, publication, and annual meeting costs were rising to astronomical heights, but membership dues, special gifts, and philanthropic and federal grants appeared not only to sustain the present range of activities but also to permit the consideration of extended services to scholars, churches, synagogues, and wider public audiences. The future looked promising, though an economic reversal could force a major curtailment of activities.

Its companion organization, the ASOR, enjoyed a similar condition of prosperity. Grants from private foundations and the federal government undergirded its publication program and provided security for the expanding activities of the Jerusalem School and the Amman center. The Cypriote government extended an invitation to establish an institute at Nicosia. Here also the prospects were bright.

Issues

What was the state of the discipline at the end of a hundred years of research? We may examine the way several contributors to the *Journal* in the seventies viewed the situation, noting issues and concerns as they identified them.

President James Muilenburg in 1968 rehearsed some of the limitations inherent in the strict practice of form criticism methodology. He urged recognition of the unique, individualistic factors in literary composition beyond what is common to all representatives of a given genre and proposed a rhetorical criticism to supplement form criticism (88 [1969] 1–13). Professor Morton Smith, the proverbial gadfly on the SBL ox, contributed an essay in 1969 under the title "The Present State of Old Testament Studies." In point of fact, it was less of a survey and more of an uproarious assault on what Smith termed "pseudorthodoxy," defined as the disposition to accommodate the work and results of historical criticism to institutional teachings and homiletical presentations which presuppose the preeminence of the Bible in a way that compromises the discipline. His own view, he continued, was that it is now clear that Israelite literature comes out of the Iron Age culture, a renaissance period, and discloses more linkages with the Mediterranean world than with the Mesopotamian world (88 [1969] 19–35).

A warning against preoccupation with the several subdivisions of literary criticism marked Harry M. Orlinsky's presidential advice to the Society in 1969, while he lamented the linguistic and historical incompetence of the younger scholars moving into the ranks of the Society. His call for the use of methodologies that would open up the social dynamics of the ancient Hebrew and Hellenistic cultures that precipitated the understandings which came to expression in their literature was to find response within a few years

---

[10] See the section on affiliate relationships in chapter VI.

in new studies in the social worlds of Israel and early Christianity (90 [1970] 1–14). To Norman Perrin, addressing the Society in 1973, echoing the emphases of German biblical scholars, especially Bultmann, the hermeneutical issue was crucial to an understanding of NT eschatology. It was precisely because Jesus understood human life as continuously confronted by God that the concept of the sovereignty of God must not be restricted to temporal terms. The kingdom symbol is a means of recognizing the manifold ways in which the experience of God can become reality. Interpreters require a deeper understanding of the function of symbols and the psychological processes of human understanding if they would uncover the meanings of these texts (93 [1974] 1–14).

Using the Chicago School in its first phase (1892–1920), Robert W. Funk in 1975 believed he had found a paradigm of liberal American biblical scholarship which, like the Harper tradition, publicly pledges allegiance to so-called scientific study of the scriptures while being covertly deferential to an unexamined presupposition of the authority of scripture (95 [1976] 1–22). "These anomalies make the SBL a fraternity of scientifically trained biblical scholars with the soul of a church. They also create certain incongruities for biblical studies in the humanities wing of the secular university." Whether or not the biblical text has any discoverable meaning for the interpreter and the interpreter's life, i.e., the question of the authority of the Bible, is the basic issue raised in German research but deliberately evaded in the American scene.

The need to recognize the divergence of text-types of the Hebrew Bible in the Greco-Roman world—a point made earlier by Morton Smith—was boldly underscored by James A. Sanders's presidential address in 1978 (98 [1979] 5–29) as he reviewed recent work in OT text and canon. New critical texts of OT writings must take into account the fluid nature of the text in the Persian and Greek periods, with standardization occurring only in the first century C.E. That raises a question about the long reign of the later Masoretic text. Even so, the exegetical practice of rabbinical interpretation, no less than that of the Church Fathers, demonstrates the continuing task of revitalizing old traditions to meet new and changed circumstances.

The centennial presidential address of Bernhard W. Anderson followed up this interest in the traditioning process in its earliest oral forms and its later elaborations in written form down to the canonical stage. He distinguished at present two approaches to biblical study each asserting primacy as the basis for a biblical theology: the traditio-historical process behind the text and the exegesis of the canonical recension itself. For Anderson a choice between them is false. Neither the historical Isaiah of Jerusalem nor canonical Isaiah can substitute for the other. The discovery of the theological meanings of the text requires a probing of its earliest stages as well as its final scriptural form. Both tradition *and* scripture, under the analysis of both historical and theological criticism, are required (100 [1981] 5–21).

Paul J. Achtemeier and Gene M. Tucker attempted an assessment of the discipline on the eve of the centennial meeting (*CSR Bulletin* 11 [1980] 72–74). They recognized in recent and controversial linguistic and sociological research an experimenting with new methods of approaching biblical literature to yield theological as well as historical results. Long-term competitiveness between archaeology and literature was giving way to a new realization of their complementary character in the reconstruction of ancient cultures. Achtemeier and Tucker spoke of the variety of forms of tradition now recognized to stand behind the gospels and epistles. Exciting new texts from Qumran, Nag Hammadi, and Ebla have been announced, but scholars are often badly handicapped in getting speedy access to them. New knowledge about religion in the ancient Near East must lead to a reexamination of the religion of Israel. Less work has been done, they believed, in the areas of biblical theology and ethics, although it is to be noted that dialogue is going on among biblical studies, process philosophy, and liberation theology. Biblical studies, especially in the wider sense that includes the full range of ancient Jewish and Christian literature, remain a land to be possessed.

Finally, there is fresh interest in some topics that have been neglected in the past, for example, roles of women in the ancient world, and the new approaches of modern interpreters who bring feminist perspectives to bear on the biblical texts.[11] The OT is beginning to be seen not solely as a patriarchal book but also as a reflection of the activity of women in the decisive events of Hebrew national history. The presence of feminine metaphors for deity, hitherto little noticed, is identified in the canonical literature. The Society is becoming sensitized to the way traditional English translations have assumed the masculine character of generic masculine pronouns in the Bible, when inclusive English words would be grammatically and historically accurate.[12] There is no dearth of unfinished business to test the investigative skills of the Society in the new century beginning.

It was curious that the century closed for the Society in a social context similar to its beginning. At the outset the members were struggling to assimilate the method and results of a "higher criticism" for an approach to canonical and paracanonical literature in the face of a public clamor against any threat to the inspiration and authority of the scriptures. While heresy trials and teachers' oaths might be things of the past, a resurgence of a militant

---

[11] At the centennial meeting, this was taken up in a panel chaired by Phyllis Trible, "The History and Sociology of Biblical Scholarship: The Effects of Women's Studies on Biblical Studies." See the published version of this discussion in *Journal for the Study of the Old Testament* 22 (1982) 3–71.

[12] The RSV translation committee is now at work on further revisions which, among other things, aim to eliminate masculine terminology that is not necessary for a correct understanding of certain passages. For example, Harry M. Orlinsky points out that 'îš does not always mean an individual male as it has customarily been taken; it often is used collectively and generically to mean people.

Fundamentalism, with political as well as ecclesiastical consequences, raised anew the question of whether a learned society is an arcane group whose members enjoy themselves in sealed isolation from public life or a sector that must accept responsibility for a larger world. Were its people engaged simply in the task of understanding the Mediterranean world of antiquity with special attention to religious institutions, rituals, and sacred writings? Or were they charged to pursue honest research and attempt an interface between that ancient and this very contemporary world? Moreover, there was no clear consensus of what was to be the role of biblical studies in the future of higher education. Incorporated into the inventory of themes and methodologies for research activity ahead, this moral issue of social responsibility might be the most nettlesome, divisive, and crucial of all that had to be considered.

VI

THE TRIBES OF THE DISPERSION

SBL Regional Structure

It is customary to think of the SBL as an eastern establishment both in inception and activities over most of its century-long history. While reckoning with it as a formidable force in the development of biblical scholarship in North America, those whom birth and/or fortune have placed west of Philadelphia have often felt that facing east is expected to be an acknowledgment of the fount of learning as well as an act of worship.

But in fact the story of the Society reveals a curious mixture of provincialism and catholicism in organization, leadership, and outlook from the very beginning. The whole story surely cannot be told apart from the accounts of the satellite groupings and regional activities of a membership that is broadly dispersed. While record keeping has been regrettably haphazard and incomplete, the evidence is sufficient to show that at an early date there was a minority concern lest the Society develop into a regional club restricted to the east coast, drawing its leadership from the eastern schools, and communicating only occasionally with the outlying provinces.

There is no denying of course that such an attitude did exist. We read in the proceedings of the forty-seventh meeting for December 1911 that the Council left the next meeting to be arranged for time and place with the Archaeological Institute (it was to be a joint meeting) "provided the latter meeting is held not further west than Washington, D.C." Catch the note of condescension in the report of Recording Secretary William H. Cobb in 1915 as he speaks: "Although our meetings have always been held on the Atlantic slope, many of the members reside in the interior, and a few on the Pacific coast; it may fairly be claimed that American biblical scholarship as a whole is well represented in the ranks of the Society." And we are aware that the first migration of an annual meeting beyond the east was made with some considerable hesitance and misgiving on the part of the Council members. The year was 1924 and the site of the meeting, hosted by the Chicago Society of Biblical Research and the University of Chicago, was Chicago; a return visit was made in 1932. In 1949 the Society accepted an invitation to help Hebrew Union College in Cincinnati celebrate its seventy-fifth anniversary. The home ties were breaking.

The first meeting to be held on the west coast took place in Berkeley, California, in 1968. A year later marked the first gathering outside the United States in the city of Toronto, and this despite the fact that Canadians had been represented in the membership since a year after the Society was founded. Once the Society had outgrown campus accommodations in the seventies it was inevitable that the annual meetings would be held in large hotels in principal cities. Further growth of the Society may limit assembly places to convention centers wherever they can be found in the century ahead.

From the outset, however, the membership was drawn from a slowly widening geographical base. The intrepid group of eight who met in the study of Philip Schaff on 2 January 1880 and determined to organize a Society of Biblical Literature and Exegesis hailed from the northeastern states of New York, Pennsylvania, New Jersey, and Connecticut. In addition scholars from Massachusetts schools were among the group of eighteen who attended the first meeting on 4 and 5 June of that same year. The earliest membership roster of thirty-five includes persons teaching and serving pastorates in all of these states and in New Hampshire. A year later, membership was drawn from beyond New England and the middle Atlantic states to include New York, eastern Ontario, Ohio, and Illinois. There were no geographical limitations for membership or for the place of meeting fixed by the constitution. At the first meeting in New York City a paper was read that had been prepared, Dr. Gardiner's record states, "by the late Rev. Robert Hutcheson of Washington, Iowa." A review of the membership four years later shows that already scholars from Tennessee, South Carolina, Virginia, Kentucky, and Ohio were qualifying for membership. And within the first decade, the range had extended to include Illinois, Kansas, Nebraska, Wisconsin, Iowa, Ontario, and California.

Traveling distances, however, made it unlikely that the attendance at the annual meeting would include many from outside the immediate area. Partly for that reason and partly out of the need for opportunity to carry on discussions and to share research results, plans were made for regional consultations that would supplement the general meeting and extend the range of participation.

The revised constitution of 1889 added Article VI, which specified:

> Sections, consisting of all the members of the Society residing in a particular locality, may be organized, with the consent of the Council, for the object stated in Art. II, ["to stimulate the critical study of the Scriptures by presenting, discussing, and publishing original papers on Biblical topics"] provided that the number of members composing any Section shall be not less than twelve. Each Section shall annually choose for itself a President, whose duty it shall be to preside over its meetings, and to take care that such papers and notes read before it as the Section may judge to be of sufficient value are transmitted promptly to the corresponding Secretary of the Society. The Sections shall meet as often as they may severally determine, provided that their meetings do not interfere with the meetings of the Society.

A year later the Council reported that steps had been taken to form three such sections. At the twenty-second meeting held at Union Theological Seminary in New York on 4 and 5 June 1891, it was announced that a Chicago Section had been approved. When were the other two organized? And what regions were represented? Unfortunately, we have been unable to find any records of their existence. We have seen earlier that the Chicago Section was organized in 1891 but within two years voted to assume independent status as the Chicago Society of Biblical Research.[1] Apart from that brief span no other sections are known to have been established until 1936.

In 1934 the SBL Council acted on a proposal to organize a Midwest section of the Society. At the annual meeting of 1935 the Society authorized the establishment of a section in cooperation with the Chicago Society of Biblical Research and recommended that programs "should be under the guidance and control of a program committee, with papers presented only by invitation." With Edgar J. Goodspeed as its first president, Theophile J. Meek as vice-president, and Donald W. Riddle as secretary-treasurer, the new section held its first meeting on 30 and 31 October 1936 at the Oriental Institute, University of Chicago. Eleven major papers were presented before a group that numbered 150. At the meeting of the parent Society two months later, Riddle reported a total of 262 members enrolled in the section. These meetings were held jointly with the Middle West Branch of the American Oriental Society and the Chicago Society of Biblical Research. That practice of concourse with cognate associations became common to all the regional groups and continues to the present.

The last thirty-five years mark the period of greatest expansion in the membership and sectional organization of the Society. In 1941 there were only three sections: Midwest, Canadian, and Pacific Coast, the latter organized that very year. By 1956 there were five and the Council made some decisions on geographical boundaries. At that time the Midwest area ranged from Montana, Wyoming, Colorado, and New Mexico (shared with the Pacific Coast Section) to Pennsylvania in the east, with West Virginia and Kentucky shared with the Southern Section.[2] A Committee for the Reevaluation of the SBL Sectional Organization reported in 1968 that there were seven sections and advised that geographical factors must be subordinated to considerations of population density and dispersion and the localization of SBL members in particular areas in determining the size of the sections.

The sections grew rapidly; in the period from 1969 to 1972 six were added. Visiting the Council meeting of the Southern Section in 1969 at the University of South Carolina, Secretary Funk "was amazed to discover that the Southern Section has now become as large and as active as our national

---

[1] See H. R. Willoughby's historical sketch of the CSBR in *The Study of the Bible Today and Tomorrow* (Chicago: University of Chicago Press, 1947) ix–xvi.

[2] Prof. C. F. Nesbitt is preparing a history of the Southern Section.

body was only a few years ago." At his invitation the secretaries came together in a consultation in 1968, now known as the Conference of Secretaries, which regularly meets just prior to the annual meeting. The budget of the Society now makes a modest sum available to assist the sections (now called regions)[3] in membership cultivation and program development.

With the increase in the size of the membership, it seemed best that some of the original regions subdivide. An Upper Midwest Region was founded in 1972, and the former Middle Atlantic Region now consists of two—one in the Hudson-Delaware area and the other around Chesapeake Bay. The second oldest constituent group, the Canadian, formed in 1939, was given permission to dissolve in 1977, because many of its members had ties with other SBL regions and the virtual identity of membership with the older Canadian Society of Biblical Studies seemed unnecessarily duplicative. In the centennial year, there were twelve regional groupings from coast to coast with well-attended meetings and strong programs.[4] The Society now belonged to all of North America.

At this juncture in the history of the Society it is clear that the regions cannot be regarded as appendages to the parent body, as they may have been in the past. They are integral parts of the whole that must be reckoned with in any projections for the future. Paul J. Achtemeier speculates that regional meetings may become the centers for more specialized studies, and the annual meetings may make more place for invited speakers and sessions combined with the traditional voluntary program units. Some see the regions as essential to the preservation of participation in the democratic organization of the Society. Others note the improved quality control of proffered papers as indicative of the strength and appeal of the regional programs over the potpourri of the national programs. They favor an increased decentralization of the Society. Whatever else, the regions are integrally related to the destiny of the Society as a whole.

Affiliate Relationships

A learned society, like a person, is known by the company it keeps. In the case of the SBL it is honorable company. From the beginning, meetings have often been held in conjunction with other organizations engaged in cognate studies. Fourteen years after the founding, the Society participated in a seven-member Congress of American Philologists. In 1900 it was again one of seven participants in the Congress of Philological and Archaeological Societies assembled in Philadelphia. Over the years joint meetings have been held frequently with the Archaeological Institute of America, the American Academy of Religion, and the American Schools of Oriental Research. More

---

[3] Since 1973 these groups have been referred to as regions rather than sections to avoid confusion with the program segment of the same name.

[4] See Appendix IV, Regions.

than forty of the annual meetings have been held in concert with one or more scholarly organizations.

As might be expected the company kept has been confined usually to the immediate family, although it is noteworthy that in the earliest decades interdisciplinary relationships were more common than in the later period. Scholarly research in the humanities and the sciences has become more and more specialized with a consequent breakdown of communication among the various fields of human knowledge, and biblical research is no exception.

At the present time affiliate relationships are recognized by the Society with the following groups: American Academy of Religion (1909; reorg. 1963), American Schools of Oriental Research (1900), Ancient Bible Manuscript Center for Preservation and Research (1978), International Organization for Masoretic Studies (1972), International Organization for Septuagint and Cognate Studies (1968), and the National Association of Professors of Hebrew (1952). Several groups have been parented by the Society, notably, the American Schools of Oriental Research and the American Academy of Religion.

The story of the establishment and development of the ASOR has been told elsewhere and need not be recited here.[5] Nonetheless, the SBL story must acknowledge proudly the diligent work of Joseph Henry Thayer, who in his presidential address of 1895 called for the establishment of an "American School of Oriental Studies in Palestine." A committee of twenty-nine was appointed "to take all needful measures to bring such a School into existence and provide for its maintenance." Five years later the dream became a reality: the School for Oriental Study and Research in Palestine was founded in Jerusalem in affiliation with the SBL, the AIA, and the AOS. The original constitution was compiled from a series of resolutions passed by the SBL in 1896. With the support of twenty founding institutions, excavations began at the site of the ancient city of Samaria, under the direction of James B. Nies. Since then the School has become the single most important center for archaeological work on the ancient Near East. Additional centers at Baghdad (1923), Amman (1970) and Carthage (1975) were established as the work progressed. In 1980 the Jerusalem School, now known as the W. F. Albright Institute of Archaeological Research in Jerusalem, and the American Center of Oriental Research in Amman were carrying on busy programs, made possible by foundation and government grants. Proposals were under consideration for new centers in Damascus and Nicosia. SBL representatives have always served on the board of trustees of the Jerusalem School and since 1920 on the executive committee.

The American Academy of Religion emerged out of a Conference of Biblical Instructors in American Colleges and Preparatory Schools, which is mentioned in the proceedings of the SBL meeting of 1915, but apparently

[5] See P. J. King, *History of the ASOR* (in press).

convened first in 1908 at the call of SBL members I. F. Wood and I. J. Peritz. Sessions were held during or following the annual meetings of the SBL. In 1932 Peritz became the first editor of the *Journal of Bible and Religion*, published by the organization known as the National Association of Biblical Instructors. With the growth of departments of religious studies in private colleges and state institutions, that title became ill suited to describe the scope of teaching in the wide area of ancient and modern religions; hence in 1963 a reorganization took place in which the name was changed to the American Academy of Religion. With the exception of a four-year period, the AAR and the SBL have held their annual meetings together since 1941. Many SBL members belong also to the AAR and participate in programs of both groups at their annual meetings.

At the initiative of Kenneth W. Clark a seminar on NT textual criticism was organized with the approval of the Society in 1946 under the title American Textual Criticism Seminar (although from the outset the emphasis was almost exclusively on the NT). A few years later (1948) the seminar agreed to participate in a major international project to prepare a new and comprehensive textual apparatus to the Greek NT (above, p. 52). In keeping with the new program structure authorized in 1970, the seminar was incorporated as the Textual Criticism Seminar, affiliated with the International Advisory Committee on NT Textual Criticism and continuing its relationship with the American editorial board of the Luke Project of the International Greek New Testament Project. With the automatic expiration of the seminar's life in 1975, the group reorganized as a section to continue its activity. An OT text criticism consultation met in 1979 and 1980 in anticipation of moving into a program unit. In part OT text criticism interests are satisfied by the present affiliation of the Society with the newly organized (1978) Ancient Bible Manuscript Center for Preservation and Research, based in Claremont, which includes in its microfilm library the manuscript film collection of the International Greek New Testament Project.

Over the years the Society's work has been strengthened by its relationships with a number of kindred research organizations, among them the American Oriental Society, the Canadian Society of Biblical Studies, the Société Biblique Canadienne, the Chicago Society of Biblical Research, the Catholic Biblical Association, the British Society of Old Testament Studies, the Studiorum Novi Testamenti Societas, the International Congress of Old Testament Studies, and the Study Commission of the World Council of Churches.

Under the aegis of the ACLS, seven professional societies including the SBL organized a Council on the Study of Religion in 1969 to "initiate, coordinate, and implement projects designed to strengthen and advance scholarship and teaching in the field of religion." The *CSR Bulletin* (1972–) carries reports by SBL officers and announcements of interest to SBL members. A second publication, *Religious Studies Review* (1974–) surveys literature in the field of study. For several years, 1972–1975, the central office in Water-loo, Ontario, handled bookkeeping and membership services for the Society until they were transferred to Scholars Press in Missoula.

In the first quarter century of its history the Society maintained rela-tionships with other research societies in the humanities and social sciences principally through joint meetings. But the realization that the other groups were less interested in the results and methods of biblical research, coupled perhaps with an innate disposition toward isolationism, led the Society to cultivate an inner life, more partisan in nature, to its own detriment. An important contribution toward reversing that trend happened in 1929 when the Society became the sixteenth member of the American Council of Learned Societies. Founded in 1919, the prestigious Council today has forty-three member societies, representing the full range of the humanities and some of the social sciences.

For many years the Society was the only organization in the Council from the field of religious studies, a distinction now shared with the AAR. The Council has served the Society and the field of study in many valuable ways over the years. SBL members have served on the Committee on the History of Religions and as annual lecturers in the committee's lectureship program. They have been recipients of honors and prizes—in 1960 Frederick C. Grant was awarded ten thousand dollars for distinguished contributions to the humanities—and financial assistance in the form of travel grants and fellowships. The annual meeting of the Council in 1960 was devoted to the theme The Bible and the Humanities. Five invited papers were published under the title *Five Essays on the Bible* (ACLS, 1960); three of them were prepared by members of the Society, Erwin R. Goodenough, Morton S. Enslin, and Nelson Glueck. An ACLS grant supported the research and publication in 1971 of the study of *Graduate Education in Religion: A Crit-ical Appraisal* by Claude Welch and an advisory committee.[6] The role of the Council in the establishment of the CSR and the venture into scholarly publication through Scholars Press has been acknowledged elsewhere as well as the substantial grant of fifty thousand dollars that helped make possible the 1972 congress. The structural changes in organization and programming that set the Society traveling in new directions in 1970 were the results of the discoveries by Executive Secretary Robert W. Funk of how other learned societies in the Council were operating. The new biblical scholarship is more interdisciplinary in intention and nature. As literary criticism, struc-turalism, anthropology, sociology, and archaeology are viewed as cognate disciplines whose research methodologies and conclusions are applicable to biblical studies, it is both inevitable and necessary that biblical studies become engaged in crossover activities. The ACLS can facilitate that, but

---

[6] *CSR Bulletin* 2 (1971) 3–9; 3 (1972) 4–23; C. Welch, *Graduate Education in Religion: A Critical Appraisal* (Missoula: University of Montana Press, 1971).

other avenues that can make encounters possible with scholars in other fields need to be explored. Faculties of seminaries are not alone as victims of academic apartheid; departments of religious studies in colleges and universities have not made noticeable use of their opportunities for scholarly communication with colleagues in other fields. In this interchange, there is much to be given and much to be gained.

VII

BROTHERS AND SISTERS

Honorary Members

The 1889 constitution provided for a category of honorary membership, persons outside of the United States who were "especially distinguished for their attainments as Biblical scholars" (Art. IV). The list of 108 scholars elected by the Society over the years contains the names of some of the best known European scholars of the late nineteenth and twentieth centuries.[1] The *Journal* contains occasional notes and articles submitted by Thomas Kelly Cheyne, Eberhard Nestle, and especially Karl Budde, and others. In acknowledgment of his election to membership in 1922, Rudolf Kittel dedicated the final volume in his *Geschichte des Volkes Israel* (1929) to the Society. Kurt Aland inscribed his study of infant baptism, *Die Säuglingstaufe im Neuen Testament und in der alten Kirche* (1961), "To the Society of Biblical Literature and Exegesis in warm appreciation of my election as honorary member." The second volume of Claus Westermann's *Commentary on Genesis, Chapters 12–50* (1975) is dedicated to the SBL.

Occasional lecturing visitations of these honorary members have enriched the annual programs of the Society and served to strengthen an international scholarship beyond national and political restrictions. One remembers, for example, the visits of Oscar Cullmann and Rudolf Bultmann in 1959 and Gerhard von Rad in 1960. Scholarship in all the main branches of human knowledge recognizes only one, indivisible world.

It is appropriate to note here the enormous indebtedness of the Society to a considerable number of European scholars who have made the United States and Canada a second home and have worked in the Society as active members. To name a few is to be reminded of what they have meant and continue to mean to the guild: Markus Barth, Arthur Vööbus, Kendrick Grobel, W. Woellner, Otto Piper, Erich Dinkler, Bertil Gärtner, Helmut Koester, Dieter Georgi, Krister Stendahl, Gösta W. Ahlström, Ernest Findlay Scott, James Moffatt, F. J. Foakes-Jackson, Kirsopp Lake, J. Y. Campbell, T. R. Glover, Reginald Fuller, Nils Dahl, Norman Perrin, W. D. Davies. The list is only a sampling. In a letter to the writer, W. D. Davies recalled his early

---

[1] See Appendix II, Honorary Members.

experiences in America in the fifties and the consciousness of immediately feeling "at home" in the Society: "This aspect of the life of the SBL as traditionally forming a point of transition or adjustment between American and European scholarship needs to be recognized in this and in other broader ways."

The internationalizing of American-Canadian biblical scholarship was in process from the inception of the Society. Many of the early members had done graduate study in the universities of Germany, France, Switzerland, and Great Britain, and some of them devoted considerable time to making German theological literature in books and periodicals available through translations to their students. A regular feature of the first annual meetings was the oral reviews of recent European literature in the field. That process was extended by the acceptance into active membership of scholars emigrating from European countries.

Although it is often charged that American and Canadian scholarship has been only a feeble echo and repetition of scholarly views originating elsewhere, especially in Germany, a more thorough assessment will put to doubt that naive judgment. In any event, there has been a growing self-consciousness and spirit of independence in American-Canadian scholarship since the last World War. So much so that one executive secretary could observe that North American scholarship has been virtually untouched by German research since World War II. Increasingly influential today are Israeli biblical scholars and archaeologists. New directions rather than rehearsals of the views of others are being marked out.

Membership Profiles

For those statistically minded it may be noted with merciful brevity that the first fifty years of its history saw the Society in a slow growth process. In the semicentennial year membership had reached 450 with the greatest gains coming in the twenties. In sharp contrast the second half century has witnessed a veritable explosion—thousands of new members swelling the ranks to a total of 4,936 by 1980, with maximum growth of 2,100 occurring in the last decade.[2]

Of more interest and meaning than gross figures are the profiles of the burgeoning community over the years. A few illustrations may suffice. One notes that the circle of New England gentlemen of the original eighties included Caspar R. Gregory of Leipzig; A. L. Long and G. Washburn of Constantinople, Turkey; A. D. Hail of Osaka, Japan; and H. C. Thomson of San Luis Potosi, Mexico. The practice of an open membership has continued over the years; today a substantial number of scholars around the world hold relationship with the Society.

---

[2] From 1889 to 1951 a system was employed to give each member a serial number indicating the order of accession as well as the year of election.

From the outset, Canadian scholars were represented. The Reverend Canon Maurice S. Baldwin of Montreal held pride of place, received into membership in 1881. For nearly forty years the Canadian Section was an important link in the chain of regions—notwithstanding the unpremeditated humor of regarding that vast Dominion as a region. Though representing less than 10 percent of the total membership, Canadians have contributed five presidents to the leadership of the Society: Theophile J. Meek, Fred V. Winnett, Frank W. Beare, R. B. Y. Scott, and Harry M. Orlinsky, the latter two of whom were transplants to educational institutions in the United States. The double portion of a Canadian president presiding over the first meeting held in Canada proved too overwhelming for Frank W. Beare, who, like Zechariah, was struck dumb by the occasion. Fortunately another Canadian, Harry M. Orlinsky, never without a word, became Beare's voice at the business meeting. (Zechariah had only a writing tablet.)

Jewish scholars early made their presence felt in the life and affairs of the Society. Rabbi Marcus Jastrow of Philadelphia became a member in 1886 together with Rabbi Gustav Gottheil and his son Richard J. H. Gottheil. The younger Gottheil became president in 1902. Morris Jastrow, Jr., joined in 1891. It would be impossible to conceive of the Society apart from dominant figures like Max L. Margolis, Julian Morgenstern, Nelson Glueck, Ralph Marcus, Louis Finkelstein, Solomon Zeitlin, Harry M. Orlinsky, Jacob Neusner, or H. Louis Ginsberg—to single out a few from the many. In recent years, with the extension of research interests into Judaism of the Greek and Roman periods of Palestine, younger Jewish scholars are finding new opportunities for collaborative studies with colleagues. The centennial year program, for example, listed the following research teams currently at work: Masoretic Studies, Septuagint and Cognate Studies, Early Rabbinic Studies, Targumic Studies, Qumran, Pseudepigrapha, Jewish Christianity, and Hellenistic Judaism.

We have noted already the increasing role played by women in the life and work of the Society, still disproportionate to their numbers in professional teaching ranks in colleges, seminaries, and universities across the country today. Fourteen years after its founding, the male bastion was breached with the election of Anna Ely Rhoads (listed later as Mrs. William C. Ladd). Two years later Rebecca Corwin of Mount Holyoke College joined the Society followed by Mary E. Woolley of Wellesley College in 1898. From approximately the turn of the century, small numbers of women were regular participants in the Society. Most of them were employed to teach biblical studies in women's colleges. Though records are not complete, it appears that Eleanor D. Wood was the first woman to present a paper before the Society, reading in 1913 on "The Weliyeh of Bedriyeh at esh-Shâphát." A scanning of the membership lists of later years identifies such prominent and published scholars as Laura H. Wild, Lucetta Mowry, Margaret B. Crook, Mary E. Andrews, Mary Ely Lyman, Silva Lake. Louise

Pettibone Smith, who joined the Society in 1915, published a study on "The Messianic Ideal of Isaiah" in *JBL* 36 (1917) 158–212. She served as Secretary in 1950–1951, but she had been preceded on the executive committee by Mary I. Hussey of Mount Holyoke College, who held the post of treasurer from 1924 to 1926. At ninety-three years of age in the centennial year, Professor Smith was the only living scholar of twelve whose names were identified with awards made to contemporary scholars at the anniversary banquet in six categories of professional achievement. With the rapid increase in the number of women in clergy and teaching posts during this last decade, the next century of the Society's history will be shaped by both women and men in the range of research activity and in administrative leadership.

The character of the membership may also be defined in terms of inter-confessional and ecumenical relationships. Conservative scholars were solicited and welcomed from the outset, though the advocates of the new liberalism, in the tradition of Nathaniel Taylor and the Beechers, formed the ruling spirit in research and discussion. Nonetheless, scholars like Princeton's Benjamin B. Warfield, N. B. Stonehouse, John Gresham Machen and, more recently, A. T. Robertson and Carl F. H. Henry have shared in the life of the Society, which has steadfastly eschewed a party line over the years. The emergence today of a new scholastic conservatism in biblical studies, distinguished from Fundamentalist views, presents a fresh opportunity in the minds of many members for a productive dialogue on the nature and authority of scripture as well as on the historical and philological issues. We have already observed the debate on the legitimacy of this problem reflected in a number of presidential addresses.

In the late fifties Catholic scholars were actively involved in the regional programs. The encyclical *Divino Afflante Spiritu* of Pope Pius XII, promulgated in 1943, encouraged Catholic scholars to accept and apply the principles of the so-called higher criticism in biblical study. In the years following this, growing numbers of Catholic scholars began to participate in the Society. Official delegates were exchanged with the Catholic Biblical Association in 1959. The Council appointed an ad hoc committee in 1963 to explore a closer relationship between the Catholic Biblical Association and the Society; a year later John L. McKenzie became the first representative of the CBA to the SBL. In the last two decades Catholic scholars have become mainstays in the research projects of the Society, and several have been distinguished leaders of the guild—John L. McKenzie (president, 1966), George W. MacRae (executive secretary, 1975–1976), Raymond E. Brown (president, 1977), and Joseph A. Fitzmyer (president, 1979).

Clergy as well as academics have been represented in the membership from the earliest days of the Society, not simply as auditors but also as full participants, contributing scholarly studies in the meetings from time to time. A review of the rolls discloses well-known figures of the hierarchy, for example, Methodist Bishop Ivan Lee Holt, who was voted into membership in 1908, and Greek Orthodox Archbishop Iakovos, who qualified in 1945.

Such relationships among Jewish and Christian scholars, conservative evangelicals and liberals, Catholic, Orthodox, and Protestant scholars have enriched the camaraderie of workers in this field of knowledge and assuredly have advanced the search for truth, which has been largely unhampered by denominational labels, doctrinal differences, and partisan loyalties. As might be predicted, this kind of collaboration developed earlier and has proceeded further at local levels in the regional groups, a guarantee of its durability.

VIII

OF THE MAKING OF BOOKS

Commentaries and Translations

The quality and value of a scholarly society must be measured finally by the character of its research work and the dissemination of it through publishing as the principal form of scholarly communication.[1] This may be tested by the encouragement it gives individual members to produce scholarly writing and by the publishing programs developed by the Society itself.

The influence of the SBL on the creative output of individual members is sometimes intangible, but by their testimony many have recognized the stimulation of the Society to their research programs. H. J. Cadbury often referred to the inspiration the meetings gave him to improve his scholarship. We have noted earlier the involvement of members in the earliest days of the Society in collective enterprises such as the Ellicott Commentary for English Readers, the Schaff-Lange *Commentary on the Holy Scriptures*, the International Critical Commentary, the Moffatt NT Commentary, the Interpreter's Bible, *The Interpreter's Dictionary of the Bible*, the Harper's NT Commentaries, *The Jerome Biblical Commentary*, and Hermeneia—a Critical and Historical Commentary on the Bible, the latter a direct outgrowth of planning begun in the NT Colloquium. Serials such as the *Journal for Theology and Church* and *New Frontiers in Theology* were designed in discussions within the Society. Most of the twenty-six scholars who developed the monumental *Beginnings of Christianity* were SBL members.

In the area of Bible translations and revisions, the Society has been well represented. Its members served on the American Committee of Revision of the Authorized Version, which gave counsel on the Revised Version of 1885 and produced the American Standard Version in 1901, regarded by many as the best Bible of all time in its faithfulness to the Hebrew and Greek originals. H. J. Cadbury once observed that in a certain sense the American Revision Committee begat the Society: about half of the original members served on the committee, thirteen to be precise. Jewish members were involved in the development of the American Jewish Version in 1917 and *A New Translation*

---

[1] A provocative restatement of this axiom with a discussion of journals and books appears in the ACLS publication, *Scholarly Communication* (Baltimore: Johns Hopkins University Press, 1979).

of the Torah According to the Masoretic Text in 1963. The Society was well represented on the Committee of Thirty-One, the so-called Standard Bible Committee, and the Advisory Board that resulted in the Revised Standard Version of 1952. The editorial board that translated the Confraternity of Christian Doctrine's edition of the Bible published in 1966 included Roman Catholic scholars with joint membership in the Catholic Biblical Association and the SBL. New translations and revisions of the scriptures in the light of new manuscript finds and archaeological evidence and exegetical aids will continue to engage American biblical scholars in the future.

The Journal

"The Journal" said Corresponding Secretary George Dahl in his 1928 report, "stands as a bulwark of American Biblical scholarship and, to a real degree, as its index. It provides a channel through which creative thought may find expression." Recently one of the transplanted British scholars wrote, "The JBL gives to the SBL a profound influence on European scholarship. This is of immense importance." With commendable self-confidence, the Council voted at the fourth meeting on 29 December 1881 to print a Journal and Proceedings, with directions to print papers read at the June meeting in full in the amount of five hundred copies. With that instruction the first volume of the *Journal* was born, distributed to members and available to the general public at a cost of three dollars for the year.[2] The following year it was ruled that the Council, acting as an editorial committee, should select the papers to appear in the *Journal*. Some concern about appearance and preservation problems must have led to the Council's empowerment of the secretary several years later "to improve the quality of the paper of the Journal as he saw best."

From the outset the *Journal* set a high standard in articles and typography. With amusement members heard the secretary in 1916 read a communication from the Third Assistant Postmaster General of the United States refusing to give the *Journal* second-class rates "on the ground that it was not scientific." They knew better.

The *Journal* appeared annually from 1882 to 1905 (but in 1886 and 1887 it was semiannual); semiannually from 1906 to 1911; quarterly from 1912 to 1914; and quarterly or semiannually since 1916. At first papers, like this history, knew no bounds. Ezra Abbot's "Remarks on Rom 9:5" in volume 1 (1881) ran to sixty-seven pages. Secretary Hinckley G. Mitchell's "The Preposition *el*" extended to seventy-seven pages (with a concordance). Restraints had to be imposed both on the time for reading, usually a half hour, and on the length of the printed text. In addition to papers published in

---

[2] Proceedings and abstracts of papers read at the first two meetings in 1880 were printed in a pamphlet under the title, *The Society of Biblical Literature and Exegesis*. They were reprinted in *JBL* 50 (1931) xxiv–xlix.

full the *Journal* early began the practice of including abstracts of other papers presented at the meetings. Brief notes were also included. The all-time record holder for articles and notes contributed was Paul Haupt (president, 1906), whose name appears over seventy-five pieces. From 1880 through 1960, full accounts of the annual meeting proceedings were included, with reports of officers and delegates, and for many years, a membership roster, new members, regional reports, and memorial minutes. Since 1961 these materials are no longer found in the *Journal* to the relief of the editor but to the dismay of the historian. Abstracts and titles together with some reports have appeared since 1970 in a pre-meeting booklet known as the *Book of Abstracts*, but one must search other sources, the *CSR Bulletin*, *Scholia*, and occasional mimeographed material, to learn about the organizational life of the Society. With the advent of critical book reviews beginning in volume 55 (1936), the *Journal* extended a valuable service to scholars. In leaner years of scholarly contributions, it has been said that to the European and the American scholar the book review section alone was worth the price of the *Journal*.

The outbreak of hostilities in Europe in 1914 threatened the publishing of the *Journal*, but through the war years Haag-Drugulin Company of Leipzig continued the printing begun in 1913, though volumes 33 (1914) and 34 (1915) were delayed in shipment for many months. Despite the inconvenience the contract was renewed and the Leipzig firm continued to print the *Journal* until 1935, when a long and happy relationship began with Maurice Jacobs and the Jewish Publication Society of America and later with the Maurice Jacobs Press. The contract was extended for the next thirty-five years, its termination marked by a testimonial banquet to Dr. Jacobs at the 1970 annual meeting. Since then, Scholars Press has been the publishing agent.

A long line of eminent scholars has shaped the editorial policy and established standards that have brought the *Journal* to a position of distinction in scholarly literature.[3] Among those who served five years or more at the exacting post of editor have been George Foot Moore (1889–1894), David G. Lyon (1894–1900), Max L. Margolis (1914–1921), George Dahl (1922–1929, 1934), Erwin R. Goodenough (1935–1942), David Noel Freedman (1955–1959), Morton S. Enslin (1960–1969), Joseph A. Fitzmyer (1971–1976), and John H. Hayes (1977–). Of them all, Morton Enslin identified himself with the *Journal* for a decade in a colorful and competent manner that won both accolades and criticisms. The raspy-voiced, iron-willed editor was convinced that the editorial policy must "center on philological and historical aspects of biblical study rather than on theological or homiletical" and he never deviated from it. Though some questioned the exclusion of theological or ethical interests (he himself wrote a major study on the ethics of Paul), there

[3] See Appendix V, Editors of the *Journal of Biblical Literature*.

was an admiration and affection for Enslin that has made the Enslin epoch a memorable one in the history of scholarly publication.

In more recent years the wise guidance and remarkable and skillful editing achievements of Joseph A. Fitzmyer have brought this periodical to a position of excellence that has won international acclaim. "In our country there are numerous religious publications but in its field the *Journal* stands alone in its record of the ranges and the results of biblical scholarship." With that appreciative judgment by an SBL member there is common concurrence. The indexes of O. H. Gates (vols. 1–40), Ralph Marcus (vols. 41–60), T. H. Gaster (vols. 60–79) and John C. Hurd (vols. 80–99 forthcoming) facilitate a mining of the collection of essays and reviews. The *Journal* now has a junior partner. *Semeia* is defined as "an experimental journal for biblical criticism." Begun in 1974, it features frontier studies in structuralist criticism, hermeneutics, oral tradition, literary criticism, literary analysis from a psychoanalytic perspective, and group studies of special literary types, such as gnomic wisdom, miracle stories, pronouncement stories, and apocalypses. Often cast in the esoteric vocabulary of advanced linguistics, the essays have been dubbed by some as "academic glossalalia." But a sober judgment will recognize here the experimental work of highly trained scholars exploring alternatives to historical criticism in the interpretation of ancient texts. The text as text, not simply as an expression of a particular cultural circumstance, requires dissection into its constituent parts for literary classification and the disclosure of potentialities of meaning.

In 1931 editor Carl H. Kraeling proposed a series of Beihefte to the *Journal*. The idea was readily accepted, but efforts to secure financing failed until 1946 when the monograph series was inaugurated with C. C. Torrey's *The Lives of the Prophets*. To date twenty-six volumes have appeared.

Concerns about scholarly communication and publication in the face of the crisis posed by astronomical printing costs by commercial houses and the reluctance of commercial houses to handle limited editions of technical works led to an inquiry into alternatives by a CSR task force in 1971. Some societies in the humanistic disciplines had already begun to experiment with publishing ventures of their own, a more daring breakaway than that of the university presses some years earlier. The report of the task force the following year articulated the problems clearly and called to attention the changing roles of learned societies. They recommended that the member societies of the Council "explore and develop ways to serve their constituencies as publishers, not only of journals and monograph series, but of dissertations, collections of essays, books of all kinds."[4] Without doubt the most enthusiastic and energetic advocate of this expansion of the SBL's role as publisher was a member of the task force, Robert W. Funk, who was then executive

---

[4] *Scholarly Communication and Publication* (ed. G. W. MacRae; Missoula: University of Montana Press, 1972) 12.

secretary of the Society. He had challenged the Council in 1969 to consider ventures in micro-publication to meet the needs of the Society beyond what its publishing program had ever been able to do in the past. Approval was given in 1971 to develop a program which may be said to have been launched with a Festschrift offered to Norman Perrin by the members of the NT Colloquium, *Christology and a Modern Pilgrimage*, edited by Hans Dieter Betz. This was followed by a number of monograph-type studies related to the work of the SBL seminars and groups.

Scholars Press was founded in 1974, a creation of the AAR and the SBL growing out of their developing research programs and publication needs. Under the leadership of its director, Robert W. Funk, a dissertation series was inaugurated followed quickly by Texts and Translations with plans on other fronts. There was no time for a slow start. New titles were offered for sale, it seemed to many, as soon as the Society press started at the University of Montana. In the centennial year, there were thirteen publication projects serving the growing number of sponsoring societies of the Press. It was an achievement that would cause even a veteran entrepreneur to marvel. The prediction of the industry was that it would be short-lived. Theological librarians held their breath. And behind it all were the energies and the daring of Bob Funk, functioning in the kaleidoscopic roles of editor, advertiser, administrator, scholar, purchasing agent, stock boy, technician, troubleshooter, and prophet. Koheleth and Gutenberg would have been dumbfounded: In 1975 the Press was incorporated into a Center for Scholarly Publishing and Services, based at Missoula, and presently located in Chico, California.[5]

In the centennial year, the following sets comprise the publication program of the Society. The dates mark the initial volume in each case:

> Monograph Series (1946)
> Dissertation Series (1972)
> Texts and Translations
> > Pseudepigrapha Series (1972)
> > Early Christian Literature Series (1974)
> > Graeco-Roman Religion Series (1976)
> Sources for Biblical Study (1974)
> Septuagint and Cognate Studies (1972)
> Masoretic Studies (1972)
> Semeia Studies (1975)
> Seminar Papers and Abstracts (1970)
> Aramaic Studies (1976)
> General Series (1976)
> Festschriften (1971)

[5] Funk describes the history of Scholars Press in *Scholia* 9 (1979) 17–22 and 10 (1980) 18.

Genres of Religious Literature in Western Antiquity (1976)
SBL Centennial Publications (1976)
Journal of Biblical Literature (1881)
Semeia: An Experimental Journal for Biblical Criticism (1974)
Publications related to groups and seminars

Interpreting the outcomes and trends of biblical research to the general public has never been a major concern of the Society, though from time to time it has been proposed as a needed service. Others maintain it would compromise scholarly goals and impede pure scientific research, but few question the excellence and value of a popular journal like *The Biblical Archaeologist*, published by the ASOR. In the early years, many of the best-known SBL scholars, as we have seen, vigorously defended the new biblical criticism in popular ecclesiastical journals such as *Bibliotheca Sacra*, the *Baptist Review*, the *Andover Review*, the *Presbyterian Quarterly*, and others. Moreover, through the years other SBL members have skillfully shared the results of biblical scholarship with a wider audience: Ira M. Price, Charles Foster Kent, Edgar J. Goodspeed, Laura H. Wild, Julian Morgenstern, R. H. Walker, E. W. K. Mould, F. C. Grant, Howard C. Kee, Bernhard W. Anderson, Raymond E. Brown, Harry M. Orlinsky, and John Bright—to name only a few of those whose writings are known to generations of college students and the laity of church and synagogue. If, as senior officials of the National Endowment for the Humanities iterate, humanist-scholars have been guilty of elitism and discrimination, preferring their own company to that of others, there are signs of a new sense of social responsibility among the members of the guild.

IX

THE VOICE OF MIRTH

Learned societies are made up of the light-hearted as well as the heavy-headed. With some, wit and humor are studied. More often it is unintentional: the slip of speech, the ambiguity of the written word, the accretions that gather about colorful figures, half legendary, half real. Here are a few items culled from the dusty sobriety of the *Journal* or the lively, often embroidered, memories of members. They may verify that they, like Dives in Jesus' story, live "in mirth and splendor."[1]

At the June meeting of 1883 held at Berkeley Divinity School, with Willis Beecher presiding, a message was read from A. M. Shaw, M.D., inviting the Society to visit the Hospital for the Insane in Middletown. "The invitation was accepted with thanks by the Society." (This appears only in the manuscript record; it was omitted from the printed account in the *Journal*.) It must have made for a full day.

A note in volume 8 (1888) carried this apology from a distracted secretary: "The paper [of J. Rendel Harris], read in June, should have formed a part of this number; but when it was wanted, it could not be found. The author, now in the East, will probably, on his return, be able to discover its whereabouts."

Among the subscribers to the *Journal* listed in 1900 and 1901 are the Mechanics' Institute in San Francisco and the Mercantile Library in St. Louis—the marketplace attendant upon the ivory tower! And for a clue to a half-remembered or totally forgotten world, consider this advance notice of the meeting in New York City in 1896: "It is hoped that members of the Society will take dinner together on Tuesday evening at a restaurant, with which the committee has arranged, at a price of fifty or seventy-five cents each" (see also figure 6).

At times papers and titles can be a source of amusement as well as instruction. Of a paper by Prof. Beecher it was noted, "The second paper on 'The Historical Situation in Joel and Obadiah' was read by Prof. Beecher. Though longer than papers have usually been, it held the attention of the members to the end and seemed to produce conviction." It may have been sheer coincidence that at the second session President Gardiner urged the need to increase the number and quality of papers presented.

[1] Lk 16:19 (ASV).

SOCIETY OF BIBLICAL LITERATURE AND EXEGESIS.

Tuesday and Wednesday, December 28 and 29, 1897.

FIRST SESSION - - DECEMBER 28, 2.30 P.M.

The meetings will be held in Room 422 of the Columbia University Library Building, 116th Street and Boulevard, New York.

To reach the place from the south one takes the Amsterdam Avenue or the Boulevard surface line to 116th Street. One may also take the Sixth Avenue or the Ninth Avenue elevated road to 116th Street; or to 104th Street, changing there to the Amsterdam Avenue line of street cars. The cars marked Boulevard and Grant's Tomb, which pass the door of the Grand Central Station at 42d Street, go directly to the University.

The Committee of Arrangements mention (as probably the most convenient and reasonable) "The Castle," a quiet family hotel, corner of 103d Street and Amsterdam Avenue. There is a restaurant in the building, and also an admirable little restaurant in the Edinboro, directly across the street.

It is proposed that the members should dine together at the University restaurant at 6 P.M. on Tuesday. Price per plate, one dollar. But to make the dinner possible there must be thirty guests. Those who will join the party are therefore requested to send their names promptly to Rev. Dr. J. P. Peters, 225 West 99th Street, New York.

Luncheon *a la carte* may also be had at the University restaurant on Wednesday, and it is hoped that the members may take this meal together.

The sessions proposed are:

1. TUESDAY . . . . . . 2.30–6 P.M.
2. " . . . . . . 8–10 P.M.
3. WEDNESDAY . . . . . 9.30 A.M.

And a fourth session Wednesday afternoon if need be.

Yours cordially,

WM. H. COBB, *Recording Secretary.*

Figure 6. Program Announcement, 1897

Financial problems were met in various ways. In 1918 Treasurer George Dahl announced that the Society would probably run into debt during the coming year. The Council was asked to consider ways and means of meeting the deficit. On motion it was voted that the recording secretary (H. J. Cadbury) should transfer his balance to the treasurer. Whether this covered the deficit is not clear.

In times of sky-rocketing budgets it is startling to discover the simple financing of the preinflationary period. In 1944 the Pacific Coast Region "voted that the Section authorize the secretary to write to the treasurer of the SBLE requesting that the Society pay $4.59 to the Section, this being one half of the expense of the meeting which was arranged in cooperation with the Pacific Coast Association of Religious Studies." Treasurer Robert C. Dentan reported a financial crisis in 1953. The next year the Council reported that $131.90 had been raised in response to the special appeal for funds. Five years later a $2.50 increase in dues was authorized. Evidently the massive response to Dentan's appeal did not stave off the creditors.

In modern colloquial speech the title of Benjamin Bacon's paper, "Is John 14 Displaced? And What Of It?" carries a quizzical touch lost in the revised title of his published article, "The Displacement of John 14." Here are some papers read at annual and regional meetings, known only by their titles, which deserve to be remembered by name if not by content:

"Did Noah Eat the Apple?"
"Alcohol in the Bible"
"A Doubtful Sumerian Paradise"
"Mr. Goodspeed and the Ethiopian"
"How Moses Failed God"
"How Tradition Failed Moses"
"Solution of Hosea's Marital Problems by Critical Analysis"
"What Shall We Do With Document Q?"
"The New Very English NT"
"The Markan Sandwiches—Some Food for Thought: Butterbrot, Ham and Cheese, Dagwoods"
"NT Research Has No Regard for the Special Intentions of the NT, and Thus Should No Longer Be Identified with Reference to It"

Anecdotes and legends about leaders of the past constitute a treasured part of a society's memorabilia, though these are seldom preserved in archives. The memories of some of our members have brought to mind quips and comments about persons and situations that ought not be lost.

Of George Barton it was alleged that his famous book *Archaeology and the Bible* went through thirty-seven editions without any verbal changes, only the insertion of additional pictures.

C. C. Torrey inspired vivid recollections of his performances.

It was not long after this period [late 1920s] that the notorious clashes occurred at meetings of the SBL between Torrey on the one hand and Goodspeed and Riddle on the other over Torrey's views on the Aramaic origins of a number of the NT writings. Torrey, slight in stature but acid in debate, could be very peremptory in refusing further discussion with those who, he averred, knew only one of the two languages in question. After one of these jousts which I was unable to attend an observer reported to me that of the three protagonists the Society could recognize two scholars and one gentleman. Since Goodspeed was undoubtedly always the gentleman that leaves only one category undecided.[2]

A historic collision occurred at the seventieth meeting in 1934 when Goodspeed, Cadbury, and Riddle dealt with the recently published major work of Torrey, *The Four Gospels, A New Translation*, which had received an affirmative review by James A. Montgomery. Some would have it that once again "the Hellenists murmured against the Hebrews," Paul in a standoff with James—history repeating itself in a new form. Though memorable this was not the only instance of impassioned debate on scholarly issues. One might recall the rigor and vigor with which an existentialist reading of history was discussed by Morton S. Enslin, Kendrick Grobel, and James M. Robinson, or again the matter of "saving" history drawn and quartered by Enslin in rhetorical combat with Otto Piper and F. V. Filson. Nor will time ever erase from memory the devastating contentions of Solomon Zeitlin that the Dead Sea Scrolls were medieval forgeries.

A Harvard Divinity School student rejoiced over the prospect of being the only student who signed for a course with George Foot Moore, relishing the opportunity to get to know this distinguished scholar personally. Alas, for the entire term Moore entered the classroom at the appointed hour, lectured, and left without a word of conversation exchanged.

One respondent reported an old quip that Cadbury had obtained his doctor's degree by depriving Luke of his.

B. H. Branscomb's own testimony, confirmed by his students, was that he was the only American scholar who could speak Hebrew with a north Georgia accent.

Of the many stories that cluster about that scholarly giant, Robert H. Pfeiffer, one of the most delightful centers in his occasional difficulty with the English language. At the meeting at Hebrew Union College in Cincinnati in 1949, celebrating the seventy-fifty anniversary of that school, President Pfeiffer rose to announce that members who had not yet paid for their board and lodging should do so. In his own inimitable style he said, "Please don't go without settling your accounts, if you have slept here, with Miss Aaronson." One man who remembered the incident offered the appropriate comment, "It was the best and most successful presidential address ever made!"

[2] A. N. Wilder, "NT Studies, 1920–1950: Reminiscences of a Changing Discipline," *Journal of Religion* (in press).

X

SIGNS AND PORTENTS

Reviewing the history of a learned society may turn out to be an exercise in nostalgia, an act of triumphalism, or by good chance a reasonably accurate assessment of the past and a plausible estimate of things to come. Historicism can affect any examination of the past and convert the historian into antiquarian pure and simple. Not wishing such a fate, we conclude the present account with some new directions, a few already begun, others in the planning stage, as the second century opens.[1]

A variety of issues had been addressed in the first century. Established in a period that marked the beginnings of scientific historical criticism applied to the biblical materials, the Society was soon embroiled in struggles associated with the new Pentateuchal criticism. We have watched the development of archaeological research activity and observed the frequent rivalry between text and artifact as a means of discovering the past. The Aramaic question became a persistent and controversial issue in NT studies. New methodologies such as form criticism gave hope of unlocking the preliterary period and charting the history of tradition until it assumed the form of literature. Neo-orthodoxy's concern to develop theology out of the Bible as its principal source posed a problem for many scholars who feared that studies in the religion of Israel or the faith formulations of the early Christian church would compromise the objectivity of historical study and make apologists out of scholars. The result of textual and archaeological work brought an enormous amount of primary material to bear on the study of earlier forms of biblical documents and the cultures within which they arose, requiring critical assessment and the rethinking of previous conclusions. To accomplish these tasks it became necessary to revamp drastically the form in which the Society had done its work, and a new organizational structure, winning plaudits and reproaches, came into being.

---

[1] The forecasting here is perforce a composite of many views and proposals. Of special usefulness were four statements: "1980 and Beyond," in R. W. Funk's "Report of the Executive Secretary, 1968–1973," *CSR Bulletin* 4 (1973) 20–26; "The Changing Role of Learned Societies," in *Scholarly Communication and Publication* (ed. G. W. MacRae; Missoula: University of Montana Press, 1972); Paul J. Achtemeier and Gene M. Tucker, "Biblical Studies: The State of the Discipline," *CSR Bulletin* 11 (1980) 72–76; R. D. Hecht, "Research Needs in the Study of the Hebrew Bible and in the Study of Judaism," *CSR Bulletin* 11 (1980) 137, 139–145.

The centennial meeting in 1980 was deliberately designed to encourage reflection on the present state of the discipline and to anticipate some of the tasks that constitute unfinished business at the moment. To investigate approaches to the Bible by new forms of social analysis drawing upon the behavioral sciences, by language analysis using tools of contemporary linguistics, by raising afresh the basic questions of intention and meaning, and by intensifying historical and archaeological research—themes of that meeting— is to trace directions in which research is now being pursued or anticipated. In the years ahead the Society conceivably may be moving on several fronts.

(1) *Purpose and scope.* The purpose of the Society, defined first in the constitution of 1884 and enlarged and redrafted in 1962, remains essentially the same: "to promote the creation and dissemination of scholarly knowledge pertaining to biblical literature and ancillary fields." As others have noted, the formal name of the Society suggests a limitation to canonical literature. To be more accurate, it has been proposed that the name should declare the aim to study religion and religious institutions in western antiquity. But this would alter the historical focus on biblical materials. In any event the scope of the inquiry continues to widen to include para-canonical and nonbiblical religious literature of the ancient world. Nathaniel Schmidt's plea at the fiftieth anniversary that more attention be given to deuterocanonical and apocryphal literature has been met beyond his imaginings, thanks to new manuscript finds. In recent years it has become evident that there is an increasing interest in rabbinical literature and postbiblical Judaism. But the scope of inquiry as yet does not embrace adequately the literature of the early patristic period, an essential part of the context of the Christian movement. The work of Robert M. Grant is a notable and welcome exception. Just as surely the Ebla materials will push back the horizons of OT study to incorporate the second millennium B.C.E. and perhaps the late third. Widening ranges of historical research are necessary and promising.

(2) *Artifacts and texts.* Despite the acknowledged fallacy in assuming a competitive relationship between archaeology and documentary study it remains true that the analysis of texts and the digging of ancient ruins are carried on still as discrete activities. This is the more astonishing in view of the interests of the newer archaeology in such questions as population distribution, urban planning, social and religious institutions, and economic programs, and textual study's concern with cultural factors and the social-cultural matrix in which literature must be set. This virtual isolationism can continue only to the detriment of the basic task. Team research involving specialists from a variety of cognate disciplines contributing their competencies would seem to be the necessary way to proceed in the future. Such collaboration can be mutually fruitful as experimental projects already testify.

(3) *Relationships with other groups.* The problem of the learned society is a microform of the problem of the multiversity in today's higher education. How can specialized knowledge be integrated into larger configurations? How

can the multiversity become a university? It is a dismal sign of our times that the joint meetings the Society once held with other groups engaged in humanistic studies have disappeared. It is considered a major achievement these days to hold a congress of specialists in the study of religions let alone to arrange converse with scholars in folklore, languages, history, or musicology. In his introduction to the collection of essays entitled *The Study of the Bible Today and Tomorrow*, published in 1947, H. R. Willoughby pointed out the variety of disciplines and techniques now drawn upon in biblical research: documentary criticism; tradition criticism; study of the cultural environment, social function, ethics, world view, cult, and organization; apologetics; translation; manuscript study; textual criticism; religious psychology; social history; and iconography. Programs of study today and in the future are and will become increasingly cross-disciplinary in approa h. Attention is paid to rhetorical criticism, structural analysis, new forms of literary criticism, cultural anthropology, and analytic psychology. It is a disturbing paradox that this widening interdisciplinary approach occurs at the same time that the Society itself has less and less interaction with other learned societies in the humanities and the social sciences. The future holds possibilities for discovering new ways of carrying on dialogue with the humanities and social sciences beyond one official delegate's attendance at the annual meeting of the ACLS or the importing of a half dozen professors from foreign parts to speak at an annual meeting. Sovereign disciplines are just as obsolete as sovereign states in a global village.

Dialogue relationships may also move in another, albeit more controversial, direction. The renascence of theological conservatism at the outset of this second century is marked by a feature not to be overlooked; what may be termed a conservative scholasticism. This has been an element within our pluralistic Society from the very outset, as we have seen. As a vital part of American biblical scholarship the presence of this conservatively oriented intelligentsia must be acknowledged, many believe, and provision made to expand their participation in the community of debate.

(4) *Computerized research and publication.* The last quarter century has seen the introduction of vast new technologies in the printing industry which have revolutionized communication and accessibility to scholarly information. Photographic processes and computerized typesetting are developments in modern research programs that depend increasingly on computers for access to source material and the classification and storage of data. The question facing the theological librarian today is not hard cover versus soft, but microfilm versus optical disk as a means of preservation. To the new breed of scholars the use of computer terminals to retrieve out-of-the-way information and word processing machines to compose technical papers will be as natural as the reference library and the typewriter have been to their forebears. Microforms—fiche and reel—enlarge the scholar's personal library and expand enormously the capability of seminary and

university libraries. One is hesitant to predict the future of the book in its conventional form. Obviously scholarly literature of the past will continue to be consulted in the printed format in which it is preserved, whether on paper or film, but just as surely a much wider range of writing in the form of notes, reports, essays and monographs will play a large part in what happens on the scholar's desk. Computers will assist in the retrieval and correlation of data, but in the face of a knowledge explosion greater burdens than ever face the critical faculties of the researcher. There is little likelihood that the inventive and imaginative skills of the human brain will be eclipsed by the computer brain. The new technologies will expand and accelerate research processes and extend the range of availability of the results in an extraordinary way. One can only hope that the quality of the scholarly program will match the quantitative extension of the materials.

There is need to bring to completion quickly the long-delayed project of compiling an inventory of basic research instruments required in the field. Inspired by an ACLS proposal to the National Endowment for the Humanities for a long-range program to identify research tools, the CSR has been engaged in developing an Inventory of Needed Research Instruments in Religious Studies. Since the project was announced in 1973, some progress and reports have been made, but in 1980 it had not yet been concluded.

(5) *Specialization and integration.* Widening horizons of biblical research with the intensification of analysis permitted by computer-assisted work inevitably foster specialization in ever-narrowing fields of inquiry. This is already a reality, commented upon sadly by a number of senior scholars who deplore the growth of subdivisions in the annual meetings, not a few of which exhibit esoteric concerns and technical vocabularies that make communication with other specialists semi-intelligible at best. Indeed such hyper-specialization drastically reduces the number of those competent to criticize, thus weakening the community of criticism which is essential to excellence. A major problem facing the Society in its second century will be to facilitate the process of communication between groups and individuals to develop languages of synthesis rather than separation and to emphasize the larger schemes and issues that will integrate atomized research activity.

(6) *Regional groups and the national Society.* The demographic growth of the Society poses severe logistical problems about the frequency, housing, and costs of the national meetings. It is probable, therefore, that the regional groups will fulfill a greater function in the future than they have in the past. Thus far there has not been any planned program change in the regional meetings comparable with the reformation of 1969 in the parent Society. On the whole the meetings follow the traditional practice of voluntary contributions in a forum setting. Secretary Achtemeier, in his final report in 1980, speculated that the regional meetings might become centers of more specialized study and the annual meetings might make more place for invited speakers and symposiums combined with voluntary program units. Biennial

meetings of the whole Society with annual regional meetings might then prove feasible.

(7) *Teaching guild and professional society.* We have noted occasional concerns to define the public audiences to which the work of the learned society is addressed. Obviously the primary concern is with the academic community. Truth for truth's sake and the scholarly enterprise answerable to itself have been the customs of the confraternity of experts. But the ivory tower mentality and practice have been under heavy attack in recent times. In the Society this has prompted proposals to share research results with a wider public, at least with church and synagogue if not with the realms of political, economic, and social struggle. Otherwise the Society becomes (some would say, has become) an antiquarian association more closely resembling an English gentlemen's club than a laboratory. Do the Cabots speak only to the Lodges and the Lodges speak only to God? Some think so.

In a time of hurried social change, the learned society like the university must redefine the role it plays in the larger society. Neither can afford to become action training centers or think tanks in the service of major industrial, political, or ecclesiastical agencies without sacrificing fidelity to historic purposes. For biblical research to accept its agenda from the religious establishment would be intolerable, a throwback to the captive scholarship of the precritical era. But it has been said that the hermeneutical task is incomplete unless it is concerned with the contemporary meanings of ancient texts. In a time when an anticritical attitude is championed in the religious community in favor of a literalist reading of the Bible has not the Society a responsibility to enter the debate? Or does it remain aloof and distant from those who struggle to find a better way? In a culture that generally regards the Bible as an "iconic" book, to use Martin Marty's phrase, where the book is respected but unread, those for whom it is the subject of their teaching and critical study have as much responsibility, it would seem, to interpret its significance to the nonspecialist as the Shakespearean scholar has to make the Bard of Avon intelligible to the general public—the more when it is either ignored or abused. The popular *Biblical Archaeology Review, Scientific American,* and *Psychology Today* provide paradigms.

(8) *Individual and cooperative research.* The development of new and very expensive research tools such as computer hardware together with the extension of biblical scholarship into larger and larger areas confirm the decisions of 1969 to organize research work increasingly on a group basis. "If scholars are willing to sacrifice a small amount of individual glory, the future looks extremely bright for large research projects which need doing but have failed to reach completion or even to find full conception because no base for ongoing work has existed."[2]

² *Scholarly Communication and Publication,* 17.

(9) *Theological and philosophical interests.* Throughout its history the Society has unanimously espoused historical, archaeological, and philological approaches to the study of biblical literature but remained hesitant and divided on the suitability of theological and philosophical concerns. Text must be examined rigorously as text, but can it also be investigated as scripture? We have listened to presidential addresses that are sharply divided in their response to the question. Is a view of the Bible as normative for faith incompatible with the aims of scholarship? The house is and no doubt will continue to be divided, but the issue will certainly continue to be faced. It may be significant that Bernhard W. Anderson, president of the Society in its centennial year, chose to speak on "Tradition and Scripture in the Community of Faith." And the *Journal* that carried that address included a sharply critical review by Walter J. Harrelson of Brevard S. Childs's *Introduction to the OT as Scripture.*[3] Historical criticism may not be bankrupt but the question of theological meanings of tradition and scripture both in the ancient situation and in the situation of the interpreter will continue to sue for recognition.

(10) *Changing membership patterns.* The second century for the Society will certainly secure and extend the broadened base of participation introduced in the reorganization of 1969. Women will play a larger role in the presentation of papers, printed articles, and in the administrative sector. This development reflects the larger number of women teaching in the field and the changing patterns of social organization. It also results from a firm intention to encourage full and equal participation of all scholars in the common tasks. Though women were numbered on some college faculties in religious studies in the early days of the Society and some became members, they have never represented more than 8 percent of the total SBL membership. According to a study by Dorothy C. Bass, the low point was in 1970, when women totaled only 3.5 percent of the membership. It is clear, however, that the future will not be a repetition of the past. Women are entering the academe in increasing numbers and will surely influence the future of all learned societies.

Ethnic and racial minorities have been meagerly represented in the SBL. The establishment of a joint committee with the AAR on Professional Standards and Development is significant in its recognition that there is something more than an open admissions policy at stake. There is the realization that the Society has a responsibility to populate the professional species, to use its influence to assist the recruitment, training, and placement of scholars representing ethnic and racial minorities. Biblical and religious studies internationally have been dominated in the past by North Americans and Europeans. The next century may see a new global form of the discipline with scholars from the Orient, South America, and the Third World

[3] *JBL* 100 (1981) 1–21; 99–103.

taking part. To be true to its purpose and commitments the Society will use its power to help make that possible.

In a letter to Kenneth W. Clark in 1965, Leroy Waterman wrote, "I can only say that my association as a member of the SBLE has been one of the great influences in my work and life." Commented Amos Wilder, "The SBL has played an indispensable role in safeguarding the continuity of the always endangered higher disciplines of our field and its texts, and providing incentives for devotion to them in each new generation." It could not be put more simply and incisively by any of us who have shared in this community of learners and learning.

APPENDIX I

Manuscript Record of the Preliminary Meeting, 2 January 1880[*]

New York, Jany 8th 1880. Several gentlemen met by previous agreement in the study of the Rev. P. Schaff, DD. 42 Bible House, to take into consideration the formation of a Society for the promotion of study in Biblical Literature and Exegesis.

There were present Drs Briggs, Goodwin, Mombert, Schaff, Short, Strong, Washburn, and Gardiner.

The Rev. D. R. Goodwin, D.D. was called to the chair, & the Rev. F. Gardiner, D.D. was appointed Secretary.

After informal discussion, it was

Resolved: that steps be taken to form a Society of Biblical Literature & Exegesis for the purpose of promoting a thorough study of the Scriptures by the reading and discussion of original papers.

Resolved: that this Society shall consist of Prof. E. Abbot, LL.D., Prof. C. A. Briggs, D.D., Pres. Thomas Chase, LL.D., Prof. T. J. Conant, D.D., Prof. Geo. E. Day, D.D., Prof. F. Gardiner, D.D., Prof. D. R. Goodwin, DD, Rev. E. Harwood, D.D., Prof. C. M. Mead, Rev. J. Mombert, D.D., Prof. A. River, D.D., Prof. Geo. Prentice, D.D., Prof. P. Schaff, D.D., Prof. Charles Short, LL.D., Prof. P.H. Steenstra, Prof. James Strong, D.D., and Rev. E. A. Washburn, D.D., together with such other persons as may be invited by a Committee to be appointed for that purpose.

Resolved: that this Com. consist of Drs Gardiner, Briggs, Short, and Strong.

---

[*] The Historical Note included in the account of the semicentennial celebration in 1930 (*JBL* 50 [1931] ii, iii) differs in several respects from this original record.

71

Resolved: That the Society shall hold its first
meeting in New York on Friday, June 4ᵗʰ, at such
place and hour as this Com. shall determine, of
which they shall give due notice to the members.

Resolved: That this Com. be requested to secure at
least two or three brief papers for reading & discussion
at that meeting, & to mention in the notice of the
meeting the subjects of such as are likely to be offered.

Resolved: That the same Com. prepare a draft
of a Constitution & by-laws to be presented at that
meeting.   Adjourned

Frederic Gardiner, Secretary.

APPENDIX II

Honorary Members

1891	Carl Paul Caspari	1924	Karl Marti
	Thomas Kelly Cheyne		James Moffatt
	August Dillmann	1925	Bernhard L. Duhm
	Charles John Ellicott	1926	Hermann Gunkel
	Frédéric Godet		Hugo Gressmann
	Abraham Kuenen	1928	Alfred Bertholet
	William Sanday	1930	Stanley A. Cook
	Eberhard Schrader		Adolf Deissmann
	Bernhard Weiss		Martin Dibelius
	Brooke Foss Westcott		Ernst Lohmeyer
1892	F. J. A. Hort		Ernst Sellin
	J. J. S. Perowne		Burnett H. Streeter
	C. P. Tiele		L. P. Hugues Vincent
1893	Heinrich Julius Holtzmann	1932	Johannes Hempel
	Robert Payne Smith	1933	Walter Bauer
1894	A. B. Davidson		Maurice Goguel
	George Salmon	1937	Otto Eissfeldt
1895	Friedrich W. A. Baethgen		Hans Lietzmann
	Samuel Berger	1938	F. M. Abel
1896	Samuel Rolles Driver		Albrecht Alt
	George Adam Smith	1940	Paul Kahle
1897	A. Ceriani	1941	Walther Eichrodt
	Solomon Schechter		Frederic G. Kenyon
1898	Karl Budde	1942	Charles Harold Dodd
	Adolf Jülicher	1946	Sigmund Mowinckel
1904	Adolf von Harnack		Johannes Pedersen
	A. H. Sayce	1947	Teófilo Ayuso
1906	Francis C. Burkitt	1948	Thomas Walter Manson
1913	Ernst von Dobschütz		Theodore Henry Robinson
	Marie-Joseph Lagrange	1950	Rudolf Bultmann
	Julius Wellhausen		Anton Fridrichsen
1922	Rudolf Kittel	1951	Kurt Galling
	John Skinner	1952	Harold Henry Rowley
	Gustaf Dalman		Johannes de Zwaan

1955	Joachim Jeremias	1972	Günther Bornkamm
	Roland de Vaux		Jean Duplacy
1956	Giovanni Cardinal Mercati		Georg Fohrer
	Martin Noth		Torgny Säve-Söderbergh
1957	Matthew Black		Rudolph Schnackenburg
	Albert Debrunner		George Widengren
1958	Benjamin Mazar		Robert McL. Wilson
1960	Kurt Aland		Yigael Yadin
	Gerhard von Rad	1975	Karl-Heinrich Rengstorf
1961	Pierre Benoit	1976	Joseph Ziegler
1964	Willem C. van Unnik	1977	Werner Georg Kümmel
1967	Ernst Käsemann		Isaac Leo Seeligmann
	G. W. H. Lampe	1978	Charles K. Barrett
1968	Charles F. D. Moule		Dominique Barthélemy
	Walter Zimmerli	1979	Claus Westermann
1969	Oscar Cullmann		Harald Riesenfeld
	Artur D. Weiser	1980	Karl Martin Fischer
1970	Bonifatius Fischer		Hartmut Gese
	Wilhelm Rudolph		Claude Schaeffer
1971	Michael Avi-Yonah		Hans-Martin Schenke
	Herbert Braun		Eduard Schweizer

APPENDIX III

Symposiums and Collaborative Research Components of Annual Meeting Programs

1918   Critical Method in the Study of the OT
         George A. Barton, Kemper Fullerton, C. C. Torrey, A. T. E. Olmstead, Julian Morgenstern

1919   The Criticism of Acts as Related to the History and Interpretation of the NT
         Edgar J. Goodspeed, James Hardy Ropes, H. J. Cadbury, C. C. Torrey, F. J. Foakes-Jackson

1921   Eschatology
         Nathaniel Schmidt, A. V. W. Jackson, Louis Ginzberg, E. F. Scott, Benjamin W. Bacon, Frank Chamberlain Porter

1922   Primitive Christianity and Judaism
         F. C. Porter, C. C. Torrey, James Hardy Ropes, Benjamin W. Bacon, Samuel S. Cohon, E. F. Scott

1929   Backgrounds of the Fourth Gospel
         Millar Burrows, Carl H. Kraeling, G. H. C. Macgregor

1930   Palestinian Judaism in the First Century
         Louis Ginzberg, F. C. Porter, Amos N. Wilder, E. W. K. Mould

1936   Judaism and Hellenism
         Robert H. Pfeiffer, Ralph Marcus, Erwin R. Goodenough, Louis Ginzberg

1939   Ideas of Salvation in the First Century A.D.
         A. C. Purdy, H. J. Cadbury, B. Cohon, Ralph Marcus

         Form Criticism and Eschatology
         C. T. Craig, B. H. Branscomb, F. C. Grant, Carl H. Kraeling, D. W. Riddle

         Northwest Semitic Epigraphy and the OT
         H. L. Ginsberg, C. H. Gordon, Harry M. Orlinsky, W. F. Albright

1940   The Idea of God in the Ancient Near East
        L. Bull, Ferris J. Stephens, H. L. Ginsberg, Herbert G. May

1941   The Present Status of Studies in the Psalms
        Joseph Reider, T. H. Gaster, R. B. Y. Scott

1948   The Jerusalem Hebrew Scrolls
        Millar Burrows, William H. Brownlee, John C. Trever

        The Reconstruction of the Persian Period of Biblical History
        *Ralph Marcus, W. F. Albright, Sheldon H. Blank, Elmer A.
        Leslie, Robert H. Pfeiffer, William F. Stinespring*

1949   The Jewish Messiah and the Pauline Christ
        Ralph Marcus, Samuel S. Cohon, Morton S. Enslin, P. Schubert

1950   Jewish and Christian Ethics in the First Century
        John W. Flight, Amos N. Wilder, Frank Zimmerman

1951   Israelite Religion and Society Under the Judges
        *G. Ernest Wright, W. F. Albright, H. L. Ginsberg, Robert H.
        Pfeiffer*

1952   Rudolf Bultmann's Interpretation of NT Eschatology
        Paul S. Minear, Floyd V. Filson, Kendrick Grobel, P. Lehmann

1953   The Present Status of Pentateuchal Criticism
        *O. R. Sellers, J. Coert Rylaarsdam, C. A. Simpson, Fred V.
        Winnett*

1954   The Dead Sea Scrolls and the NT
        *Millar Burrows, William H. Brownlee, Sherman E. Johnson,
        William L. Reed*

1957   Problems in Biblical Hermeneutics
        *Walter J. Harrelson, James Muilenburg, J. Coert Rylaarsdam,
        Krister Stendahl*

1958   Recent Developments in the Study of the Text of the Bible
        Bruce M. Metzger, Patrick W. Skehan, Harry M. Orlinsky

1959   The Son of Man Problem in the OT, the NT, and Judaism
        *James Muilenburg, Eduard Schweizer, Samuel Sandmel, Morton
        Smith*

1960   A Letter Attributed to Clement of Alexandria and Containing
        Quotations from a Secret Gospel Attributed to St. Mark
        James A. Sanders, Morton Smith, Pierson Parker

1961   Method in Bibical Studies
        J. Moreau, David Noel Freedman, Floyd V. Filson, George E. Mendenhall

1962   Language in Biblical Interpretation
        C. T. Fritsch, James Barr, H. A. Gleason, Helmut Koester

1963   Biblical Studies and the Classics
        Krister Stendahl, Erwin R. Goodenough, Gösta Ahlström, James M. Robinson

1965   The Problem of the OT Canon
        R. B. Y. Scott, R. Murphy, Albert C. Sundberg

1966   Nag Hammadi Studies
        John L. McKenzie, James M. Robinson, Robert A. Kraft, R. A. Bullard

1967   Apocalyptic Literature and Thought
        Frank Moore Cross, Moshe Greenberg, David Noel Freedman, Hans Dieter Betz, Robert W. Funk

1968   Prophecy and Prophets in Ancient Israel
        James Muilenburg, Rolf Knierim, H. Huffmon, E. von Waldow

1969   Mythology and the OT
        Harry M. Orlinsky, T. H. Gaster, R. J. Williams, Brevard S. Childs

1970   Approaches to Bible Translation
        Lawrence E. Toombs, Raymond E. Brown, J. Philip Hyatt, Harry M. Orlinsky, Keith R. Crim

        Eschatological Language
        Martin J. Buss, William G. Doty, T. J. J. Altizer, Amos N. Wilder

1971–1980 Collaborative research has been organized about the following topics: NT Textual Criticism, Gospels, Form Criticism (Hebrew Scriptures), Paul, Pseudepigrapha, Midrash, Lexicography, Nag Hammadi, Early Christian Prophecy, Parables, Linguistics, Ugaritic Studies, Greco-Roman Religions, Social World of Early Christianity, Ancient Epistolography, Process Hermeneutic and Biblical Exegesis, NT Forms and Genres, Social World of Ancient Israel, Relationships of the Gospels, Hellenistic Judaism, Ancient Near Eastern and Biblical Law, Formation of the Prophetic Books, Hellenistic Mystery Religions, Gospel of Mark, Luke-Acts, Jewish Christianity, Structuralism and Exegesis, Pauline Ethics, Thessalonian Correspondence, Social Roles of Prophecy.

APPENDIX IV

Regions

A Chronological Listing by Organizational Meetings

Midwest, 1936
Canadian, 1939; dissolved, 1977
Pacific Coast, 1941
Southeastern (formerly Southern), 1948
New England, 1950
Southwestern, 1957
Middle Atlantic, 1958; divided into
    Hudson-Delaware, 1969
    Chesapeake Bay, 1969
Eastern Great Lakes, 1970
Pacific Northwest, 1971
Rocky Mountain-Great Plains (formerly Rocky
    Mountain), 1972
Upper Midwest, 1972
Missouri-Kansas, 1977

APPENDIX V

Editors of the *Journal of Biblical Literature**

1880–1883	Frederic Gardiner
1883–1889	Hinckley G. Mitchell
1889–1894	George Foot Moore
1894–1900	David G. Lyon
1901–1904	Lewis B. Paton
1905–1906	James Hardy Ropes
1907	Benjamin W. Bacon
1908–1909	Julius A. Bewer
1910–1913	James A. Montgomery
1914–1921	Max L. Margolis
1922–1929	George Dahl
1930–1933	Carl H. Kraeling
1934	George Dahl
1935–1942	Erwin R. Goodenough
1943–1947	Robert H. Pfeiffer
1948–1950	J. Philip Hyatt
1951–1954	Robert C. Dentan
1955–1959	David Noel Freedman
1960–1969	Morton S. Enslin
1970	John Reumann
1971–1976	Joseph A. Fitzmyer
1977–	John H. Hayes

---

* The title editor has been used since 1938. Prior to that the secretary or corresponding secretary fulfilled editorial responsibilities.

APPENDIX VI

SBL Presidents*

1880–87	Daniel Raynes Goodwin	1922	William R. Arnold
1887–89	Frederic Gardiner	1923	Max L. Margolis
1889–90	Francis Brown	1924	Clayton R. Bowen
1890–91	Charles A. Briggs	1925	Julius A. Bewer
1891–94	Talbot W. Chambers	1926	Shirley Jackson Case
1894–95	Joseph Henry Thayer	1927	Irving F. Wood
1895–96	Francis Brown	1928	Loring Woart Batten
1896–97	Edward T. Bartlett	1929	James E. Frame
1898–99	George Foot Moore	1930	William Frederic Badè
1900	John P. Peters	1931	Burton Scott Easton
1901	Edward Y. Hincks	1932	J. M. Powis Smith
1902	Benjamin W. Bacon	1933	James Moffatt
1903	Richard J. H. Gottheil	1934	Frederick C. Grant
1904	Willis J. Beecher	1935	Elihu Grant
1905	William Rainey Harper	1936	Henry J. Cadbury
1906	Paul Haupt	1937	George Dahl
1907	James Hardy Ropes	1938	Wm. Henry Paine Hatch
1908	Frank Chamberlain Porter	1939	William F. Albright
1909	Henry Preserved Smith	1940	Chester C. McCown
1910	David G. Lyon	1941	Julian Morgenstern
1911	Ernest DeWitt Burton	1942–43	Kirsopp Lake
1912	Lewis B. Paton	1944	Theophile James Meek
1913	George A. Barton	1945	Morton Scott Enslin
1914	Nathaniel Schmidt	1946	Leroy Waterman
1915	Charles Cutler Torrey	1947	Ernest Cadman Colwell
1916	Morris Jastrow, Jr.	1948	John W. Flight
1917	Warren J. Moulton	1949	Floyd V. Filson
1918	James A. Montgomery	1950	Robert H. Pfeiffer
1919	Edgar J. Goodspeed	1951	Erwin R. Goodenough
1920	Albert T. Clay	1952	Sheldon Blank
1921	Kemper Fullerton	1953	S. Vernon McCasland

---

* Years indicate period of tenure.

1954	Millar Burrows	1968	James Muilenburg
1955	Amos N. Wilder	1969	Frank W. Beare
1956	J. Philip Hyatt	1970	Harry M. Orlinsky
1957	Sherman E. Johnson	1971	Bruce M. Metzger
1958	William A. Irwin	1972	Walter J. Harrelson
1959	Robert M. Grant	1973	Norman Perrin
1960	R. B. Y. Scott	1974	Frank M. Cross, Jr.
1961	Samuel Sandmel	1975	Robert W. Funk
1962	Herbert G. May	1976	David Noel Freedman
1963	John Knox	1977	Raymond E. Brown
1964	Fred V. Winnett	1978	James A. Sanders
1965	Kenneth W. Clark	1979	Joseph A. Fitzmyer
1966	John L. McKenzie	1980	Bernhard Anderson
1967	Paul Schubert	1981	James M. Robinson

APPENDIX VII

Honorary Presidents

1969	H. Louis Ginsberg	G. Ernest Wright
1970	Paul S. Minear	
1971	Otto A. Piper	William F. Stinespring
1973	Theodor H. Gaster	
1976	John Bright	
1977	W. D. Davies	
1978	Pierson Parker	
1979	Nils A. Dahl	
1981	Ernest W. Saunders	Samuel Terrien

APPENDIX VIII

SBL Secretaries

1880–1883	Frederic Gardiner
1883–1889	Hinckley G. Mitchell
1889–1890	Charles Rufus Brown°
1890–1915	William H. Cobb
1916–1933	Henry J. Cadbury
1934–1946	John W. Flight
1947–1950	Kenneth W. Clark
1951–1952	Louise Pettibone Smith
1953–1961	Charles F. Kraft
1961	Albert C. Sundberg, Jr., *pro tempore*
1962–1965	Kendrick Grobel°°
1965	Richard T. Mead, *pro tempore*
1966	Lawrence E. Toombs
1967	Walter J. Harrelson
1968–1974	Robert W. Funk
1975–1976	George W. MacRae
1977–1980	Paul J. Achtemeier
1981–	Kent Harold Richards

° The title recording secretary was used from 1889 to 1963.
°° The title executive secretary has been used since 1964.

INDEX

Abbot, Ezra, 4, 5, 6, 7, 10, 32, 88, 105
Abel, Felix-Marie, 37, 107
Achtemeier, Paul J., 66, 70, 76, 97, 100,
    121
Adler, Cyrus, 8, 33, 35
Ahlström, Gösta, 81, 111
Aiken, C. A., 3
Aland, Kurt, 49, 52, 81, 108
Albright, William Foxwell, 38, 39, 45,
    47, 48, 53, 62, 77, 109, 110, 117
Alt, Albrecht, 37, 47, 107
Altizer, T. J. J., 111
Anderson, Bernhard W., 52, 67, 69, 92,
    102, 118
Andrews, Mary E., 83
Arnold, William R., 117
Avi-Yonah, Michael, 108
Ayuso, Teófilo, 107

Bacon, Benjamin W., 6, 11, 28, 33, 47,
    48, 95, 109, 115, 117
Badè, William Frederic, 34, 117
Baethgen, Friedrich W. A., 107
Balch, D. L., 51
Baldwin, Maurice S., 6, 83
Barr, James, 111
Barrett, Charles K., 108
Barth, Markus, 81
Barthélemy, Jean-Dominique, 108
Bartlett, Edward T., 117
Barton, George A., 8, 11, 25, 29, 46, 47,
    95, 109, 117
Bass, Dorothy C., 102
Batten, Loring Woart, 117
Bauer, Walter, 107
Baur, Ferdinand Christian, 1
Beardslee, W. A., 65
Beare, Frank W., 33, 58, 59, 83, 118

Beatty, Sir Alfred Chester, 43, 44
Beecher, Willis J., 5, 22, 84, 93, 117
Beker, J. C., 53
Benoit, Pierre, 108
Berger, Samuel, 107
Bertholet, Alfred, 35, 107
Betz, Hans Dieter, 91, 111
Bewer, Julius A., 8, 27, 31, 37, 47, 48,
    115, 117
Bissell, Edwin C., 11
Black, Matthew, 108
Blake, Robert Pierpont, 46
Blank, Sheldon H., 110, 117
Bliss, F. J., 15
Bodmer, M. Martin, 44
Bornkamm, Günther, 108
Bowen, Clayton R., 117
Branscomb, B. H., 96, 109
Braun, Herbert, 108
Breasted, James H., 33
Briggs, Charles Augustus, 3, 4, 5, 8, 11,
    12, 17, 18, 22, 105, 117
Briggs, Emilie Grace, 8
Bright, John, 92, 119
Brown, Charles Rufus, 12, 121
Brown, Francis, 4, 5, 11, 12, 22, 27, 117
Brown, Raymond E., 67, 84, 92, 111,
    118
Brown, William Adams, 8
Brownlee, William Hugh, 44, 110
Bryan, William Jennings, 32
Budde, Karl, 7, 33, 35, 81, 107
Bull, L., 110
Bullard, R. A., 111
Bultmann, Rudolf, 31, 81, 107
Burkitt, Francis C., 107
Burrows, Millar, 37, 44, 109, 110, 118
Burton, Ernest DeWitt, 6, 33, 117

Buss, Martin J., 111
Buttz, Henry A., 22

Cadbury, Henry J., 25, 35, 37, 38, 39, 47, 48, 49, 55, 87, 95, 96, 109, 117, 121
Campbell, A. F., 65
Campbell, J. Y., 81
Carlyle, Thomas, 1
Case, Shirley Jackson, 22, 46, 47, 117
Caspari, Carl Paul, 7, 107
Ceriani, Antonius, 107
Chambers, Talbot W., 27, 117
Chase, Thomas, 105
Cheyne, Thomas Kelly, 7, 81, 107
Childs, Brevard Springs, 52, 102, 111
Clark, Kenneth W., 32, 47, 52, 62, 78, 103, 118, 121
Clay, Albert T., 47, 117
Clermont-Ganneau, C., 15
Cobb, William H., 24, 33, 73, 94, 121
Cohon, B., 109
Cohon, S. S., 110
Collins, Adela Yarbro, 66
Colwell, Ernest Cadman, 49, 117
Comte, Auguste, 1
Conant, T. J., 105
Conder, C. R., 15
Cone, Orello, 17
Conzelmann, Hans, 48
Cook, Stanley A., 107
Corwin, Rebecca, 8, 83
Craig, C. T., 47, 109
Cramer, M. J., 11
Crim, Keith R., 111
Crook, Margaret Brackenbury, 83
Cross, Frank Moore, 66, 67, 111, 118
Cullmann, Oscar, 81, 108

Dahl, George, 25, 88, 89, 95, 115, 117
Dahl, Nils, 81, 119
Dalman, Gustaf, 35, 107
Darrow, Clarence, 32
Darwin, Charles, 1, 33
Davidson, A. B., 107
Davies, W. D., 81, 119
Day, George E., 4, 5, 13, 105
Debrunner, Albert, 108

Deissmann, Adolf, 33, 107
Dentan, Robert C., 49, 95, 115
Dibelius, Martin, 31, 46, 107
Dillmann, August, 7, 107
Dinkler, Erich, 81
Dobschütz, Ernst von, 23, 35, 107
Dodd, C. H., 107
Doty, William G., 59, 111
Driver, Samuel Rolles, 4, 107
Duhm, Bernhard L., 107
Duplacy, Jean, 108
Dwight, Timothy, 4, 10, 32

Easton, Burton Scott, 22, 46, 117
Eichrodt, Walther, 54, 107
Eissfeldt, Otto, 107
Ellicott, Charles John, 7, 107
Emerson, Ralph Waldo, 2
Enslin, Morton Scott, 47, 48, 53, 61, 79, 89, 90, 96, 110, 115, 117
Epp, Eldon Jay, 66

Faraday, Michael, 1
Feeley-Harnik, Gillian, 66
Filson, Floyd V., 54, 96, 110, 111, 117
Finkelstein, Louis, 83
Fischer, Bonifatius, 108
Fischer, Karl Martin, 108
Fitzmyer, Joseph A., 67, 84, 89, 90, 115, 118
Flight, John W., 33, 110, 117, 121
Foakes-Jackson, F. J., 46, 81, 109
Fohrer, Georg, 108
Frame, James E., 8, 47, 117
Freedman, David Noel, 89, 111, 115, 118
Fridrichsen, Anton, 107
Fritsch, C. T., 111
Fuller, Reginald, 81
Fullerton, Kemper, 25, 46, 109, 117
Funk, Robert W., 24, 49, 52, 53, 58, 59, 60, 63, 66, 67, 69, 75, 79, 90, 91, 97, 111, 118, 121

Galling, Kurt, 107
Gardiner, Frederic, 3, 4, 7, 8, 9, 11, 13, 17, 27, 61, 74, 93, 105, 106, 115, 117, 121

Kahle, Paul, 107
Kapelrud, Arvid S., 49
Käsemann, Ernst, 108
Kee, Howard Clark, 92
Kent, Charles Foster, 8, 33, 92
Kenyon, Frederic G., 46, 107
King, Philip J., 16, 77
Kitchener, H. H., 15
Kittel, Rudolf, 81, 107
Knierim, Rolf, 111
Knight, Douglas A., 66
Knight, Douglas M., 49
Knox, John, 67, 118
Koester, Helmut, 53, 81, 111
Kraeling, Carl H., 51, 90, 109, 115
Kraeling, E. G., 42
Kraft, Charles F., 121
Kraft, Robert A., 52, 58, 111
Kuenen, Abraham, 7, 17, 107
Kümmel, Werner Georg, 108
Küng, Hans, 66

Ladd, Mrs. William C. (see Anna Ely
    Rhoads)
Lagrange, Marie-Joseph, 23, 33, 107
Lake, Kirsopp, 46, 47, 81, 117
Lake, Silva, 83
Lampe, G. W. H., 108
Lange, John Peter, 13
Leach, Edmund, 66
Lehmann, P., 110
Leslie, E. A., 110
Lietzmann, Hans, 107
Lister, Joseph, 1
Lohmeyer, Ernst, 107
Long, A. L., 82
Longfellow, Henry Wadsworth, 8
Lyman, Mary Ely, 83
Lyon, David G., 8, 12, 33, 35, 89, 115,
    117

Macalister, R. A. S., 15
McArthur, Harvey, 33
McCasland, S. Vernon, 117
McCown, Chester C., 47, 54, 117
McCurdy, James F., 4
McGaughy, Lane C., 63
McGiffert, Arthur Cushman, 8, 17, 33

Macgregor, G. H. C., 109
Machen, John Greshen, 84
McKenzie, John L., 84, 111, 118
MacRae, George W., 63, 66, 67, 84, 90,
    97, 121
Manson, Thomas Walter, 47, 107
Marcus, Ralph, 47, 83, 90, 109, 110
Margolis, Max L., 33, 37, 47, 83, 89, 115,
    117
Marti, Karl, 107
Marty, Martin, 66, 101
Marx, Karl, 1
Mathews, Shailer, 6, 8
May, Herbert Gordon, 58, 110, 118
Mazar, Benjamin, 108
Mead, C. M., 105
Mead, Richard T., 49, 121
Meek, Theophile James, 48, 75, 83, 117
Mendenhall, George E., 33, 111
Mercati, Giovanni Cardinal, 108
Merrill, Selah, 15, 16
Metzger, Bruce M., 44, 45, 49, 110, 118
Meyer, Martin A., 22
Meyer, P. W., 53
Miller, J. Hillis, 66
Minear, P., 110, 119
Mitchell, Hinckley G., 17, 18, 22, 88,
    115, 121
Moffatt, James, 46, 48, 81, 107, 117
Mombert, Jacob I., 3, 105
Montgomery, James A., 23, 29, 31, 34,
    35, 37, 46, 96, 115, 117
Moore, George Foot, 6, 11, 12, 13, 18,
    27, 33, 35, 47, 53, 89, 96, 115, 117
Moreau, J., 111
Morgenstern, Julian, 25, 47, 48, 50, 52,
    53, 58, 83, 92, 109, 117
Mould, E. W. K., 92, 109
Moule, C. F. D., 108
Moulton, Warren J., 26, 37, 46, 47, 117
Mowinckel, Sigmund, 107
Mowry, Mary Lucetta, 33, 83
Muilenburg, James, 47, 49, 68, 110, 111,
    118
Munck, Johannes, 48
Murdock, W., 59
Murphy, Roland E., 111